TOUCHING THE HEARTS OF STUDENTS

Characteristics of Lasallian Schools

George Van Grieken, FSC

The photo on the front cover shows a statue of St. John Baptist de La Salle by Lejeune, done in 1951. The statue stands at the birthplace of De La Salle in Reims, France.

Published by Christian Brothers Publications
4351 Garden City Drive, Suite 200, Landover, MD 20785-2248

Library of Congress Catalog Card Number: 99-74631

ISBN 1-884904-18-1

CONTENTS

*Do you have such faith that it is able to
touch the hearts of your students and
to inspire them with the Christian spirit?*

*This is the greatest miracle you could perform,
and the one that God asks of you,
since this is the purpose of your work.*

De La Salle

Introduction: What This Book Is About

This is a book for all of those individuals—administrators, Brothers, teachers, coaches, staff, students, parents, alumni, and others—who find themselves asking the question, "What does it mean to be Lasallian?" During the course of my twenty-five years in and around Lasallian schools, it is the one question that has increasingly become the first asked and the last answered. A teacher with many years experience at a school will ask it with bewildered frustration during a faculty meeting on the school's identity. Another teacher, just new to the school, will conversationally ask it with genuine curiosity in the parking lot while chatting with an administrator. A Brother will quietly ask it after others have asked the same question of him. A board of trustees member will voice it with directness during a board discussion about the goals of the school. A parent will ask it with real interest during an open house event or while appealing a decision made by the administration. A student will ask it with complete openness during a class discussion on why this school is special or while preparing a schoolwide prayer service commemorating Saint John Baptist de La Salle.

In each case, the point is the same. Suddenly, because of particular circumstances and situations, the question of Lasallian identity is no longer an academic one. Now it makes a difference. But what is that difference? What is it about this school, this program, this teacher, this student, this lesson, this response, this gesture, that gives it a Lasallian flavor? Why not simply call it all "Christian" and stop there? Didn't the founder of the Brothers, after all, call them the Brothers of the Christian Schools and not the Brothers of the Lasallian Schools? Why worry about what it means to be Lasallian?

In large part, I agree with those sentiments. If we could have Lasallian schools that were excellent Catholic "Christian Schools" (what his schools were called in De La Salle's time) without any reference to John Baptist de La Salle or his heritage, we should be perfectly content. De La Salle would not be exactly pleased at the way his name has come to be identified with a particular style of education. His primary concern was that the schools "run well" and that its graduates were able to become mature, responsible members of society and the church. Nevertheless, in the course of establishing "Christian Schools," De La Salle and the Brothers devised a methodology and a foundational perspective about education that were quietly revolutionary and that became very successful.

Schools don't pop up value-free. In an educational community of individuals where the point is to direct, suggest, discuss, share, challenge, and evaluate ideas, the convictions that one holds about students, teachers, the teacher-student relationship, the activity of teaching, and the school in general make a real difference. Is it a difference one can measure accurately? I don't think so. Is it a difference others value? It is when you listen to the graduates that come back for reunions. Is it a difference that will determine if a Lasallian school without Brothers will survive? Not necessarily. Is it a difference that will determine if a Lasallian school without Brothers remains Lasallian? Most definitely.

The point behind this book is that being a Lasallian school does make a real difference with real consequences. Those graduates or longtime faculty members or Brothers who are asked about what makes a school Lasallian often first respond with a blank expression, and then they tell a story about Brother X or about student Y or about situation Z. This book provides the main story behind all the individual stories of Lasallian experience. It tells the story of De La Salle and the educational movement he continues to inspire today.

Simply put, this book addresses the three main questions that underlie the question of Lasallian identity:
- Who was this Saint John Baptist de La Salle?
- What educational vision and practice came about because of his influence?
- What does that vision and practice look like today?

After some basic information about the state of Lasallian schools in the United States in recent times, a short outline of the life and times of John Baptist de La Salle will be provided. This is followed by a fairly detailed presentation of De La Salle's educational vision and practice, using his own words wherever possible. The last section presents a contemporary articulation of Lasallian spirituality and how that spirituality might be lived out in the educational communities that call themselves *Lasallian* today.

Each of the book's sections, in order, speaks to the question of Lasallian identity. One cannot fully appreciate what Lasallian spirituality is like today without knowing who De La Salle was or what his educational vision looked like. The identity of De La Salle and the vision and practices he brought about enable us to understand and implement his charism here and now. The more we know about De La Salle and his ways, the more we will be able to speak about ourselves and our ways in terms that give substance to the adjective *Lasallian*.

This book is based on a doctoral dissertation written at Boston College in 1995 under the patient direction of Professor Thomas Groome and with the insightful contributions of Br. Luke Salm, FSC, and Fr. Joseph O'Keefe, SJ. It has been extensively edited so as to make it more readable for a general audience. All footnotes have been eliminated or incorporated into the text. Large sections of material have been summarized or eliminated for the sake of brevity, outside references have been reduced to the bare minimum, and all quotations from De La Salle's works are without specific reference. Copies of the original work, with the full text, references and footnotes may be obtained from the author (see the bibliography). Where references are given in this book, they are in this form: (Name of the author [or title], year published, page number or specific section of the citation). The books are listed in the bibliography.

Grateful acknowledgement is given to the many Lasallian scholars who have endured my patient probing over the years and who continue to fan the flames of Lasallian studies, especially Br. Michel Sauvage (who planted a spark in me over twenty-five years ago), Br. Gerard Rummery, Br. Luke Salm, Br. Miguel Campos, Br. Augustine Loes, Br. William Mann, Br. Jeffrey Calligan, Br. Frederick Mueller, and Br. Dominic Everett. Personal thanks as well to Mr. Gery Short for his ongoing collaboration and leadership in the area of Lasallian mission awareness, and to Br. Robert Wickman for reading virtually everything I've written in preparation for this work, balancing my insights with a realism based upon years of Lasallian administrative experience, and giving the kind of support that only a good friend can provide. The credit for the substance of this work belongs to all of them, while the errors or omissions are mine alone.

♥

1

The Context for Lasallian Identity

The Lasallian charism has passed through a great deal of history during the last three hundred years. The original context within which it arose is vastly different from that of today. A person from seventeenth-century France would be entirely lost in today's world. Yet it is within today's world that the Lasallian charism is established, having spread from about one hundred Brothers in twenty-three communities at the time of De La Salle's death in 1719, to one thousand Brothers in France at the time of the French Revolution, to a handful after the revolution, to some fifteen thousand by the end of the nineteenth century, to about seven thousand in recent years.

In 1998, there were 6,694 Brothers. Of these, a total of 2,777 Brothers worked with 64,687 partners and 784,061 students among 904 educational institutions throughout the world. In the United States alone, there were 969 Brothers. Of these, a total of 187 Brothers worked with 3,123 partners and 69,311 students among 94 educational institutions. (Non-traditional or informal apostolates are not included in these statistics.)

Such statistics make it clear that the vast majority of teachers in Lasallian institutions (93%) are men (45%) and women (48%) who are engaged in the mission of Lasallian education alongside the Brothers (6%) and other religious or clergy (1%). Taking a quick look at the contemporary educational context of the Lasallian charism will help establish why the issue of Lasallian identity is such a vital one.

LASALLIAN SCHOOLS TODAY

In the United States, Lasallian schools are Catholic schools, and as such they have evolved in a parallel fashion with other Catholic schools. The Second Vatican Council's call for the renewal of religious communities according to the Gospel, the charism of the group's Founder, and the signs of the times, introduced a process of adaptation for both Lasallian schools and the religious life of the Brothers that continues today. The highlights of this process are fairly well known to those Brothers and others who lived through this time of profound transformation.

Up until Vatican Council II, Lasallian schools followed fundamental pedagogical guidelines established in various written documents and developed through supplemental efforts. However, "until 1966, schools conducted by the Christian Brothers in the United States operated under goals which were remarkably similar to the goals of Catholic schools in general with some specification of distinctive goals in the *Rule* [of 1947] and in the goal statements of 1943." (Mueller, 1994, p. 163–164) The 1967 *Declaration* on the Brother in the world today began to recapture early Lasallian educational characteristics, and the *Rule* of 1967 recovered key aspects of schools based on the teachings of De La Salle. A concerted effort in North America to formulate key characteristics of Lasallian schools led to the 1986 document *Characteristics of Lasallian Schools,* by the Regional Education Committee of the Christian Brothers.

At the same time, a number of practical factors has led to substantial changes in the way the Brothers see themselves as members of the church and of the worldwide educational community. Membership in the Institute has dramatically declined while responsibilities have expanded. The median age of the Brothers has continually increased. Concern for the Lasallian educational charism has led to new apostolates to the economically poor. Educational enterprises in Third World countries have met with general success and enthusiasm, leading to rapid expansion and an influx of new vocations in those countries. Most significantly, the proportion of Brothers involved in Lasallian schools, compared to the number of lay colleagues, has dramatically shifted.

Lay Colleagues in Lasallian Schools

In 1984, when 78 percent of the teachers in Catholic schools of the United States were lay teachers, it was projected that by 1995 most of the faculties in Catholic schools of this country would be entirely made up of lay people. (Bryk, 1994, p. 32) A radical turnaround in the composition of those who staff and administer Catholic schools has occurred, especially within the last twenty-five years. Whereas in 1920, over 92 percent of elementary and secondary Catholic school teachers were clerics or men and women religious, in 1990 over 86 percent of elementary and secondary Catholic school teachers were laymen and laywomen (Mueller, 1994, p. 111). Given the key role that teachers acquire in the school, this change has meant a fundamental modification of Catholic school identity.

A lay character has been part of the Lasallian tradition since its inception. De La Salle established a religious institute of laymen. He strove to form other Catholic lay teachers, individual country schoolmasters sent to him for training by their pastors, with the same foundations that shaped the educational identity of the Brothers. His *Meditations for the Time of Retreat* was written for all who are engaged in the education of youth, and his spirituality has been recommended by the church as beneficial for all church educators. Yet the Christian Schools that the Brothers established, from the seventeenth century into the twentieth century, rigorously remained the exclusive domain of the Brothers alone. If lay colleagues were present, they were looked upon as a "necessary evil," something to be avoided if possible and to be tolerated if needed.

Within this century, the Brothers' stance changed—from the prescription in the 1925 *Rule* that "the Brothers of this Institute shall not have any communication with secular persons, except in cases of well recognized necessity . . . " to the statement in the 1987 *Rule* that "the Brothers gladly associate lay persons with them in their educational mission." From directives requiring that secular teachers in the schools not be admitted to the Brothers' house and that the Brothers not become too familiar with them, the Institute has come to welcome the inclusion of eighteen Lasallian lay people and two religious women as consultants during the course of the 1993 General Chapter. "A Message on Shared Mission" was generated at this same General Chapter that established the goal of moving towards the full involvement of our lay partners in the work of Lasallian education. In 1946, policy required "the immediate removal of the feminine element employed in certain places in consequence of the war . . . [and the] progressive reduction of the lay element" in the schools. But in 1981, the General Council advocated that the Brothers "be more associated with [lay colleagues] and give them leadership within the framework of our common mission and responsibility." Clearly the turnabout has been radical and deep.

Beginning in the late 1950s, the Brothers, as expressed by a former Superior General, came

> to realize that lay teachers have come into our schools to stay, and that we owe them a debt of gratitude for their admirable spirit of cooperation and for the enlightened zeal they manifest in the cause of Christian education. . . . [P]upils have the inspiring example of the Brothers ever before them, but what they learn to take for granted in a religious usually appears more striking in "one of themselves."

The *Declaration* and the 1967 *Rule* set the tone for the future by expressing appreciation for lay colleagues and by urging their full participation in the schools. Various circulars and letters from the Superior General recognized the difficulties posed by this new relationship with lay colleagues, yet all were determined to help realize the rightful and equal role of the laity in the teaching ministry. The challenge was to reverse the trend that brought lay colleagues into Lasallian educational work but paid less attention to their involvement in the Brothers' mission, and still less to their formation in terms of foundational Lasallian commitments.

The 1987 *Rule,* the normative guidelines after thirty years of development, declared that "The spiritual gifts which the Church has received in Saint John Baptist de La Salle go far beyond the confines of the Institute which he founded." Various lay Lasallian movements around the world were seen as a "grace from God" renewing the Institute's vitality. A circular that followed the General Chapter of 1986 called on the Brothers to no longer see themselves as "proprietors" of the work and mission but rather as sharers in a common ministry. Despite the frustration and demoralization experienced by many Brothers who long for the "good old days" and by many lay colleagues who long for the full realization of equal partnership, the development of lay involvement became the Institute's most significant dimension since Vatican Council II.

It was at the General Chapter of 1993 that this providential movement of the expansion of the Lasallian charism broke wide open, as the major theme of the Chapter became focused on the concept of "shared mission." Recognizing "the indispensable necessity of our Lasallian partners in the mission of the Institute . . . [a] deep feeling caught hold of the Chapter that sharing the mission is an unmistakable sign of the times . . . . We realize more than ever that shared mission is a way of life for us in the Institute." In both *A Message About the Shared Mission to the Worldwide Lasallian Family from the 42nd General Chapter* and in an extensive report on shared mission, the delegates articulated the history, the theology, and the future challenges and opportunities of sharing the Institute's mission as expressed in the 1987 *Rule,* "to give a human and Christian education to the young, especially the poor." Each person, Brother and lay colleague alike, is called to accomplish that mission according to his or her own vocation. While the Brothers "should be readily available for priority projects for the educational service of the poor where others either cannot or will not go," all who participate in the work of Lasallian education should "rejoice in the rich diversity of our respective vocations and the responsibilities these imply." Through various resolutions, invitations, and newly established structures, this concentration on sharing the mission "will be a priority at all levels in the Institute during the next seven years."

As a result of the sentiments expressed and the resolutions passed at the 1993 General Chapter, an Institute-wide document was published by the General Council in 1997 entitled, "The Lasallian Mission of Human and Christian Education: A Shared

Mission." This document provides the background, context, history, and vision for understanding the common mission of human and Christian education that is being shared among Brothers and colleagues as partners in that mission. The document drives home the fact that Brothers and lay educators are co-responsible for a common mission. The Lasallian mission of human and Christian education is by its very nature today a shared mission. It is a mission of the Church, something that comes through the mediation of the Holy Spirit and is actualized through the very being of the Church, a Church that consists of laity, religious, priests, and bishops. ("A Shared Mission," p. 86) When we speak of "shared mission" we do not speak of a mission that the Brothers "had" and now "share"; we speak of a mission that the Church "has" and "shares" among all of her members, a mission that the Lasallian heritage has lived out, still lives out, and continues to live out with a particular nuance, a characteristic flavor, a specific character.

It would be one thing if the Brothers were blindly advocating an interest in "shared mission" among educational partners who had little interest in such a thing. As it turns out, however, more and more educators in the schools are hungry for a genuine, practical educational spirituality that has stood the test of time. Such an interest is indicated by the increasing popularity of programs that specifically address Lasallian identity and Lasallian character—the Buttimer Institute of Lasallian Studies, the Lasallian Leadership Institute, District Workshops for Schools, Faculty Orientation Programs & Retreats, and so on.

Within Catholic education in general, there has been, in respect to schools, a shift of religious order involvement from "ownership and control" toward "inspiration and vision." More and more private schools are actively pursuing an affiliation with some religious educational tradition and heritage that will orient, focus, and shape their educational identity.

The use of the words "Lasallian" and "shared mission" among schools within the Lasallian heritage has seen such an increase that many are finding their use more frustrating than helpful, rightly insisting that we should know what they mean before we use them too quickly. (The present book is written in partial response to this.) In this respect, it is important to remember that using the words "Lasallian" and "shared mission" is not as important as authentically living out the reality that those words represent in a particular place and time. It is also significant that more recently the term "shared mission" is used less and less; rather, the simple term "mission" or "Lasallian mission" is the preferred way of speaking about the educational activities that are in fact being shared every day in Lasallian schools throughout the world.

In many ways, of course, the effective mission of Lasallian education has been shared with others for quite some time, although without the direct enthusiasm reflected in the 1993 General Chapter's documents. As a matter of incontrovertible fact, laymen and laywomen currently are the major formative influence in schools affiliated with the heritage of De La Salle. In 1958, the faculties of Lasallian high schools in the United States were composed of 72 percent Brothers and 28 percent lay colleagues. In 1998, these same schools were composed of 6 percent Brothers and 92 percent lay colleagues (with 2 percent other religious and clerics). At the same time, the large majority of administrative positions were held by lay colleagues. Providence

The 42nd General Chapter met at the Generalate in Rome from April 5 to May 15, 1993. For the first time in our history, eighteen lay men and women who share in the Lasallian mission, along with two religious sisters, also participated as Consultants.

seems to be speaking quite clearly and loudly, despite the well-concealed reluctance of many to accept its guidance, let alone step forward with bold enthusiasm.

While in Asia lay colleagues have long stood beside the Brothers in their work, in the United States their integration has been anything but smooth. Brothers felt that the accessibility of Christian education would be threatened by salary requirements and that elitist trends would displace religious ones. Lay teachers distrusted the Brothers who retained control over pay scales and advancement and who seemed to enjoy special privileges not available to the lay faculty. Lay faculty members recognized that their lifestyles and responsibilities might mitigate against a total commitment to the Lasallian school and that some teachers may stay at the schools for pragmatic reasons rather than religious ones.

The Lasallian schools that are presently undergoing major changes in terms of faculty personnel, style of administrative leadership, direction of educational policy, and financial priorities are at a point where the issue of Lasallian identity may at first glance seem to be superficial, something that can be talked about if there is time. In fact, however, the reverse is the case. The issue of Lasallian identity is the key issue here. Recall Jesus asking his disciples first, "Who do others say that I am?" and then, "And you? Who do you say that I am?" The question of identity informs, forms, and transforms what one thinks, how one acts, where one moves, why one goes this way instead of that way, and so on.

A familiarity with De La Salle and his educational vision and practice will lead to suggestions, decisions, and plans that reflect particular commitments. These commitments, presented in the latter part of the book, lead to the stories that we will tell when others ask us what a Lasallian school is like. And those stories are ones that Lasallian partners throughout history, both Brothers and colleagues alike, will be able to recognize and confirm.

An Encouraging Sign

Each Lasallian institution suffers from a certain kind of myopia or parochialism, brought on by sheer necessity, that centers the attention of its administration, faculty, and educational community on the immediate pieces of daily school life. It is difficult to genuinely realize that another Lasallian educational institution holds similar priorities, values, and basic commitments. When students meet together for leadership retreats, Lasallian Youth gatherings, or common service projects they are often surprised to hear the same Lasallian prayer responses from others or listen to educational experiences very similar to their own experiences. The fact that this regularly occurs on many levels among students, faculty, administrators and others involved in a Lasallian school's life is an encouraging sign. It means that there is something here that bears a true identity.

The deep nature of that common shared identity was strongly brought home to many people at a recent District-wide Convocation on the West coast. Six hundred Brothers, faculty, administrators, Board members, students and others involved in various schools and educational projects gathered to reflect on what they were about and how they could move forward. As part of that Convocation, a professional video producer spent two months traveling to the many places throughout the District and around the world where the Lasallian mission was being accomplished and where the District had been able to make a contribution of personnel or finances. Many hours of film were edited down to a few short five or six-minute video segments that poignantly expressed the common experience—the common mission—among Lasallian institutions on the West Coast and in Sri Lanka, Pakistan, India, Vietnam and Kenya. This video professional, who had produced videos for national network programs and multi-national corporations, asked if he could say something at the Convocation where the videos would be shown. Although not a public speaker, he felt compelled to stand up and address the six hundred representatives of the District-wide Lasallian educational community.

> I want to start by saying thank you; and I really mean that. This was an enormous undertaking for us and a large number of people helped make it come to pass at every institution around, it seemed, half the planet that my sound man and I ended up getting to. Last June I

got a phone call, and a couple of weeks later, I was standing on a dusty street in Pakistan, looking around, saying, "What happened? How did I end up here? How did we end up here?" 52 shooting days, 50,000 miles, 7 countries, 56 hours of videotape, over a thousand still photographs, in places that look wildly different from each other; different colors of people, different faces, different costumes and dress, different languages. We have heard "Let us remember that we are in the holy presence of God" in seven different languages in the course of this trip. But in that difference, there was a sameness everywhere, absolutely everywhere. It is remarkable to see how much every image that you see on this screen looked like you. These people who look so different are doing exactly the same work, everywhere. It is remarkable to see how similar it is and how powerful and wonderful it was for someone who knew nothing of this, to watch this process happening here and in all of those other countries. Absolutely inspiring, touching, moving, powerful stuff, absolutely wonderful—and as a cameraman, what fun to shoot; those faces, those kids. Absolutely spectacular, just simply wonderful. Every face you see here has been you, every single one. It's you doing that work there as well as here. All over the place. You should be very proud of what you do. It is wonderful work. It is absolutely wonderful work. You are, of course, educators, Lasallian educators, and you certainly educated my sound man and me in the course of this project.

It is very clear that the *experience* of a common identity is solidly established among Lasallian institutions around the world. Without this, any effort to articulate a Lasallian identity would have nothing to stand on. It is finally the experience of identity that brings forth the effort to articulate that identity. Because when the outlines of that identity become more clearly understood, we can be intentional and deliberate in doing better what we already do so well. This is something that John Baptist de La Salle would

have understood—indeed, he lived it out in his life—and it is
something that we will experience as we better understand and articulate the mission that is ours.

Brothers, faculty, administrators, Board members, students and others
involved in various schools and educational projects gathered at a
West Coast District Convocation in October, 1998.

♥

2

De La Salle's Life and Times

John Baptist de La Salle never wanted to start a religious order, let alone an educational movement that would in 1950 have him declared as the special patron of all teachers of youth by Pope Pius XII, or that would in 1998 have 67,763 educators teaching in over 80 countries of the world. All he wanted to do as a young man was to become a good priest working for the church in seventeenth-century France. Yet one thing led to another, and before he realized it he was involved with a group of rather slovenly men of marginal intelligence running a couple of gratuitous, parish-based inner-city schools for streetwise ten to fourteen-year-old boys whose expertise in gambling, rough-housing, and petty vice overshadowed any thought of reading, writing, and Christian responsibility. He writes much later on:

> I had imagined that the care which I assumed of the schools and the masters would amount only to a marginal involvement committing me to no more than providing for the subsistence of the masters and assuring that they acquitted themselves of their tasks with piety and devotedness. . . . Indeed, if I had ever thought that the care I was taking of the schoolmasters out of pure charity would ever have made it my duty to live with them, I would have dropped the whole project. . . . Indeed, I experienced a great deal of unpleasantness when I first had them come to my house. This lasted two years. It

was undoubtedly for this reason that God, Who guides all things with wisdom and serenity, Whose way it is not to force the inclinations of persons, willed to commit me entirely to the development of the schools. He did this in an imperceptible way and over a long period of time so that one commitment led to another in a way that I did not foresee in the beginning.

So how did this all come about? We won't go into all of the fascinating details, but the highlights can be easily enough presented. For those interested in a more complete picture of the life of De La Salle, the most accessible biography in English is *The Work Is Yours,* by Luke Salm, FSC, and the most exhaustive biography in English is *De La Salle: A City Saint and the Liberation of the Poor through Education,* by Alfred Calcutt, FSC.

DE LA SALLE'S WORLD

De La Salle grew up in a world without electricity, cars, telephone, TV, radio, or computer. He couldn't simply flick a switch to have light, couldn't go fairly quickly almost anywhere he wanted to go, and couldn't communicate instantly with almost anyone in the world. His was a world of candlelight, horse carriages, walking, letter-writing, frequent illness or death, and firm social classes or limitations.

This was the age of King Louis XIV, the "Sun King" who ruled France with an iron, if clever, fist. It was an age when social standing, good manners, benefices, political intrigue, and grand living were the rule. And that was just in the church. The State had all of this plus it was engaged in one war after another, taxed the populace as much as the people could tolerate, followed a system of governance and justice that had as many exceptions as it had applications, and for a time built up France's status to that of a "superpower," although economically the Dutch were the dominant players. Along the way, the poor remained quite poor, many of the rich became even richer, and a good number of the more industrious artisans, shopkeepers, and minor officials managed to have an increasingly influential voice in public affairs.

Economically, Europe was a mixed bag of "haves" and "have-nots," with certain countries or areas within a country enjoying prosperity while other areas languished. Custom duties had to be paid at each town or province through which products passed. As a result, smuggling was an accepted way of life. Almost all European economies, being based largely on agriculture, experienced frequent economic crises, especially if a particular year's crops failed. When these crises happened, starvation and widespread epidemics would be sure to follow.

Two-thirds of the over twenty million French people of the time lived in the countryside in small villages of two or three hundred. These villages provided the agricultural base on which the country stood. One-fifth of France's farmland was occupied by a host of small farms that supported four-fifths of the population with their harvest. People in both the countryside and the towns rose at dawn and retired at sunset. Six or seven day work-weeks were the norm, with each work-day lasting up to fourteen hours. The common daily diet consisted mainly of bread and meat. The only vegetables that were consumed were the herbs garnishing the beef, mutton, pork, or fowl.

In towns, the guilds *(corps de métiers)* were powerful fraternities of tradespeople such as butchers, barrel makers, carpenters,

A painting depicting a bread and poultry market in Paris in 1660.
Note the style of dress worn by the men of the time.

masons, writing masters, and others. They might be considered similar to the corporations of today, although their advocacy posture bears more resemblance to that of today's unions. Each guild had regulations that governed their particular trade, specifying the number of shops, apprentices, clerks, and other details. They ensured common standards, such as they were, and safeguarded an effective monopoly.

After the sporadic economic efforts of earlier Ministers of Finance, many of whom succeeded primarily in accumulating vast amounts of personal wealth, Louis XIV's finance minister, Jean-Baptiste Colbert (1641-1683), initiated and subsidized basic and essential industries and soon turned France's economy around, increasing the government's wealth substantially. But deficit spending as a result of the Dutch War (1672–1679) caused his plans to unravel, and France's financial difficulties again dominated the economic scene. It was primarily this economic downturn that provided the backdrop for De La Salle's work.

Taxation was a main source of income for the various governing bodies, but its collection was neither consistent nor fair. One author writes that the tax system in seventeenth-century France "would seem to have been designed with the sole object of ensuring a minimum return to the King at a maximum price to his subjects, with the heaviest share falling on the poorest section of the population." (Lewis, 1978, p. 63) Who paid taxes and how much each one paid was based more on one's social class than on anything else. The peasants, urban poor, and lower classes were burdened with the bulk of the government's taxation. At every emergency, the main direct tax, the *taille,* was increased. Its only limit was "the government's estimate of what a province could bear without revolt . . . " (Lewis, 1978, p. 64) The hardship of taxation had led to the Fronde riots in Paris, and taxation would remain a volatile issue among the French people.

On the social scene, after 1680 and the rise of Colbert from the bourgeoisie to the state's highest offices, birth no longer was the only measure of a person's worth in France. Merchants, wealthy artisans, bishops, and city council members all jostled for positions of influence. The upper bourgeoisie, which included the De La Salle family, consisted of nobles, royal officials, the professions, and the wealthiest master-craftsmen. These lived a fairly comfortable life-style. The artisan class of the time was part of the "petite bour-geoisie." These were the independent master-craftsmen, the small

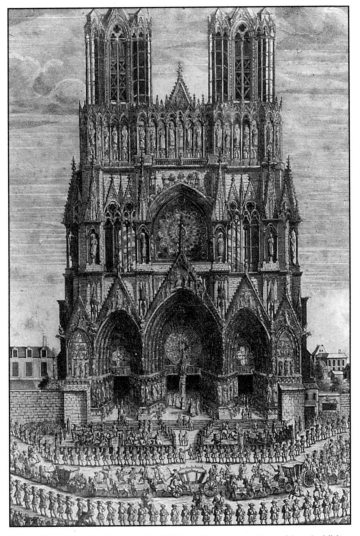

The Cathedral of Reims in 1722 at the coronation of Louis XV.
De La Salle served as canon of this cathedral from 1667
until he resigned in 1683. (Engraving by Chiquet)

traders, and the shopkeepers who were able to weather difficult times, remaining relatively well-off but having no voice in the running of the town's affairs.

The poor of the seventeenth-century were in a vastly different situation from that of the poor in today's Western culture. Today's standard considers as "poor" all those who cannot afford the minimal comforts enjoyed by the lowest wage-earner. Such a standard would include most people of seventeenth century France. The standard of that time, however, considered as "poor" all those who had neither steady income nor savings for times of unemployment; that is, no real security for surviving an economic crisis. The "destitute," moreover, were a social category encompassing all those whose insecurity was a continual way of life. The destitute rarely ate enough, or survived winters without heat, and didn't get married until they were able to afford a family, usually after the age of thirty. Both the "poor" and the "destitute" were at the mercy of the seasons and harvest, regularly experiencing periods of unemployment and semi-starvation.

The poor did have a few resources at their disposal. Each parish had a register of the poor within its boundaries and accepted gifts or money for them. Monasteries regularly distributed bread and soup, providing shelter to wandering beggars. A poor tax was levied on all non-indigent citizens for the purpose of sustaining the poor. Judicial magistrates, instead of sending wealthy individuals to prison, might impose heavy fines on them, directing such funds to various agencies for the benefit of the poor. All schoolteachers were to accept poor schoolchildren without charge, although the limited clothing, language, and hygiene of the poor (not to mention the minimal costs involved in purchasing school supplies) kept most of them away. In the general scheme of seventeenth-century French society, the poor and destitute occupied a position of dependence and inferiority that is difficult to appreciate fully.

Religiously, France in the seventeenth-century was a country in which the church and the State were intimately linked together. The Catholic Church owned one-fourth to one-third of the national wealth. From the time of the decline of the Roman Empire's influence in France, the church had exercised its strong administrative structure within the country. As the first of the three estates into which the kingdom was divided, the church enjoyed great prestige. Along with its status, however, the church performed many important and vital social functions. All works of charity, including education, were under the church's control. Clergy and religious built the buildings, provided the personnel, and often financially underwrote the schools, hospices, and hospitals that provided what we might call social services today.

From the King down, the church's involvement was wide and deep. Louis XIV considered himself a devout Catholic and strove to remain as such. He made proposals regarding religious matters to clerical assemblies and requested their financial and moral support in social and economic schemes. He selected bishops by sending the pope a list of favorites. Church officials presided together with lay magistrates in the supreme law courts. Police routinely enforced fasting and abstinence during Lent, arresting butchers, for example, who were open on Fridays. Every organization and religious community needed "letters patent" (similar to today's Articles of Incorporation) from the King in order to have legal status. People looked to the parish as the country's basic religious and administrative center. Every village was, first of all, a parish, and the priest was second in rank behind the local nobleman. It was through the parish that most French people encountered the substance of their government.

Church life was intense and extensive. Saint Sulpice in Paris had its first Mass at 4:00 a.m. every day, with many people in attendance. Twenty-five memorial Masses a day would not be uncommon. Daily Mass was also part of the normal routine in parish charity schools, as it came to be in De La Salle's Christian Schools.

In French spirituality, growing interest in contemplation and mysticism was joined with the Catholic affirmation of uniting faith with action. The ideal of personal renewal through religious devotion and works of mercy started by Italy's Oratory of Divine Love in 1497 was quickly followed by other religious groups dedicated to the reform of the clergy and to doing good works. The "French School of Spirituality", associated with Cardinal de Bérulle (1575–1629), influenced De La Salle's early seminary training, as is evidenced in De La Salle's writings.

This French School of Spirituality stressed the necessity of one's personal *kenosis* (self-emptying) in order to be filled with Christ. The Christian made explicit acts of faith in the "principal Christian mysteries" (the Trinity, the Incarnation, the Redemption, and so on), incarnating the very being of Jesus by adopting actions and interior attitudes similar to those Christ first brought to reality by His every deed, His every feeling, His every outlook; in terms of their depth and effect, His every "mystery." By entering into Christ's dispositions, one entered into Christ's mystical reality of salvation and thereby came to act, and to be, more and more like Him.

This was also a time when Jansenism's serious and rigorous outlook on the economy of grace working within corrupt human nature led to a rather negative view of the possibility of salvation. By making original sin and the absolute, constant need of grace the focal point of Christian belief, the idea of an uphill battle in pursuit of salvation came to the fore. Concurrently, Quietism arose through a distrust of human initiative in the economy of grace, preaching passivity of soul, particularly with regard to prayer; and Gallicanism insisted on the independence of the French bishops from Rome, denying the personal infallibility of the pope, and severely limiting papal authority over temporal rulers.

Yet, while he was greatly influenced by French spirituality and the various ideological movements of his time, De La Salle

> uniquely blended a number of dimensions present in the French School into his new community: the apostolate, the importance of education, a sense of the needy, the element of service, and so on. As the French School, among its male representatives, had stressed the priesthood as the experienced example of commitment to Jesus, so now La Salle stressed the apostolate of teaching as an expression of Jesus. (Thompson, 1989, p. 81)

Simply put, De La Salle applied to primary school teaching and lay teachers what the ideological momentum of the Council of Trent had effected in seminary teaching and priests.

On the educational front, before and during the time of King Louis XIV, education was discussed as heatedly as theology and politics. France had a well-established school system geared mostly for the non-poor, consisting of schools, colleges, and universities run by religious orders, secular priests, and lay professors. Education in France was under church control, and essentially religious in content, inspiration, and direction. The bishop was the local superintendent of public instruction, acting through an appointed superintendent of schools who saw mainly to the financial concerns of the individual teachers under his patronage.

The Council of Trent (1545–1563) had also mandated free parish schools (on the primary level) for the poor, establishing the parish priest as the new authority overseeing the poor's religious instruction and schooling. In response to the Council of Trent's mandate of free parish schools for the poor, numerous "charity schools" were established with mixed success. Parish priests could now open their own schools, but anyone else had to have the superintendent's permission to open or teach in a primary school. Qualifications among teachers varied widely. Often they were tradesmen (cobblers, tailors, ropemakers, and so on) who gave some daily time to instructing children. Most parish schools continued to suffer from

A print by Augustin de Saint-Aubin showing typically high-spirited boys coming out of school in 18th century France.

a lack of adequately trained full-time teachers, sufficient money, and appropriate school buildings.

By the time De La Salle became involved in primary education in 1680, primary schools were widely divergent in style and quality. Primary schooling consisted of learning the main elements of education up to the age of nine. Reading was begun with Latin syllables and words, the theory being that these were easier to learn and more beneficial besides. After that, a male student might enter a *Collège* where education would continue in Latin. The first years of education could be acquired in various ways:

- Being tutored at home. This was the preferred option of the wealthy. It was also the way that De La Salle himself was educated.
- Attending a grammar school. These were primary schools connected with some university. It was presumed that education would be continued there.
- Attending choir school. Those singing in the cathedral choir attended their own school on the cathedral grounds.
- Attending a "Little School." These were taught by schoolmasters who belonged to the Guild of Schoolmasters. They were paid a modest fee by the parents

An engraving entitled "The Old Schoolmaster" by Bosse gives an example of a common school setting of the time, with one-on-one instruction and others idly occupied.

and were supervised by the diocesan superintendent
of schools.

- Attending a convent school. These were boarding and
day schools taught by nuns. Such schools were almost
always the exclusive domain for girls.
- Attending a writing school. These schools were run by
members of the Guild of Writing Masters, officially
protected by the civil authorities. They taught writing, reading, and some bookkeeping.
- Attending a charity school. These schools, operated
by the poor house or by a parish, were for the destitute; that is, those listed on the parish list of the poor.
Today, we would consider those taught in these schools
as paupers or welfare cases.

The poor in the towns and cities would rarely attend any of
these schools. A non-working child represented a lack of income
to the family, and there was little relationship between the subjects
studied in most schools and the daily concerns of working people.

The Little Schools and charity schools were schools that provided a terminal education. An average stay at these schools lasted two or three years. With some knowledge of reading, writing,
arithmetic, manners, and religious instruction, students were then
apprenticed to various trades or found work as they could. Those
tutored at home or taught in grammar schools attached to universities were expected to continue their education, and would
pursue law, medicine, or a church position.

On the primary level, educational methodology consisted of
rote memorization and recitation of lessons to the teacher on an
individual basis. While other students were either studying, engaged in some manual task, or creatively interacting with each
other (gambling was very popular), one student would be with
the teacher, displaying knowledge of the assignment. Very often,
a single room with benches and tables was the school—either a
room in the teacher's house, one rented for the purpose, or a place
supplied by the authorities. About twenty students made up a
school, all bringing their own books and writing materials. There
were no charts or blackboards since individual instruction was the
norm.

All ages and abilities were in the same room, although girls and boys usually were not taught together. Some of the schools were open only in winter, others for only three or four days a week. Attendance was inconsistent, depending on the disposition of the students or the teacher on any particular day. Corporal punishment was considered a normal part of effective instruction. Even the King had been subject to such methods by his early teachers.

The teachers who staffed the schools were little trained in pedagogy. Those staffed by clergy from recently introduced seminary training programs at least benefited from their intellectual formation, even if these clerics-in-training had never been instructed in the art of teaching or classroom management. In almost all the schools in France, there was no organized system for selecting, training, and supervising teachers after they had entered the classroom. Lay teachers taxed the parish's financial resources, and retaining them was difficult, since someone sufficiently prepared to teach in the charity school could easily make more money in some other occupation. Some had tried to establish religious congregations or confraternities dedicated to teaching boys, but none met with much success until the work of De La Salle.

De La Salle's genius lay in organizing the schools, training and supervising teachers, and adapting various educational methodologies, thereby elevating the lay ministry of teaching within the church and generally doing well what had up to that time been done poorly. Both the religious convictions which led him to see Christ in the poor and the empathy which drew him into his work for educating the poor provided the foundation upon which his view of the vocation of the Christian teacher was progressively built.

DE LA SALLE'S STORY – THE EARLY YEARS

John Baptist de La Salle was the first of eleven children born to Louis de La Salle, a magistrate in the presidial court of Reims, and Nicolle Moët de Brouillet. Two younger sisters and two younger brothers died in infancy, something not uncommon at the time. The city of Reims, with its narrow streets, multiple churches, and large central cathedral, was home to an extended family of aunts, uncles, cousins, and grandparents. From the time he was born on April 30, 1651, to the time the family moved some blocks away thirteen years later, John Baptist grew up in a stately residence near the center of this city of kings and merchants. The courtyard and the street recess leading to the family home were the places where he played with his siblings, and the house with its

This is the inner courtyard of De La Salle's childhood home, where he lived from birth until the age of fourteen.

Renaissance facade was the place where he learned how to read and write, most likely under the direction of a tutor. The nearby cathedral with its echoing ancient bells dominated the skyline as it dominated the pious practices of his family. With relatives associated with both the cathedral and with various religious orders, John Baptist's religious upbringing was thoroughly assured. At the same time, his upper-class family maintained a lifestyle in keeping with their social position, employing servants and entertaining guests on a regular basis. While not pampered, one may assume that John Baptist led a comfortable existence, encountering none of the difficulties experienced by the poor or the destitute. During those initial years, it became evident that John Baptist had inherited the integrity and professional seriousness of his father and the human qualities and virtues of his mother, who had been brought up in the most exacting practices of Christian piety.

It would have been expected that the eldest son of Louis de La Salle follow in his father's footsteps with a law career. But from his youth, John Baptist had been attracted to the life of the church. After four years of tutoring at home, having learned how to read and spell from Latin texts, he was enrolled in the Collège des Bons-Enfants, an adjunct of the University of Reims, in October of 1661. Near the end of his first year at the Collège, at the tender age of ten, John Baptist decided to aspire to the priesthood, receiving the clerical tonsure at the invitation of his distant cousin, Father Pierre Dozet, chancellor of the University of Reims. Now wearing a black cassock, John Baptist continued to excel in his prescribed course of classical studies.

In 1666, when John Baptist was almost sixteen, Pierre Dozet again favored his young cousin by resigning his benefice as canon of the Reims cathedral in favor of John Baptist. This position obligated him to attend daily office and Eucharist, participate in regular meetings of the Cathedral Chapter, and belong to the archbishop's advisory group if asked. Besides the honor and significant financial benefits of this added responsibility, such a position placed De La Salle on the fast track in ecclesiastical circles. One year later he completed his classical studies and began the traditional two-year course in philosophy. These studies were completed on July 9, 1669, when he passed a long oral examination (in Latin) on logic, ethics, and philosophy with highest honors. At eighteen years of age, he was ready to enter the University, carrying with him a master of arts degree, minor orders, and the benefice associated with membership in the Reims Cathedral Chapter.

After spending one year studying theology at the University of Reims, De La Salle moved to the Seminary of Saint Sulpice in Paris. This seminary, established by Jean-Jacques Olier in 1645, had as its goal to produce priests committed to a life of self-sacrifice and self-discipline, with zeal for the salvation of souls, especially the poor. Life was rigorous, filled with work, prayer, and silence. In fact, the overall routine of the seminary—silence, meditation, spiritual reading, reading at meals, daily examination of conscience, multiple devotions, and openness to the spiritual director, to name a few—bears a striking resemblance to the routine that De La Salle would later introduce in the training of his schoolmasters.

Soon, however, any expectations he had of leading a fairly ordinary life as a cleric came to an end. John Baptist's mother died in the final weeks of his first year at the seminary in Paris and his father died less than nine months later. As the eldest male in the family and the executor of his father's estate, De La Salle returned to Reims to take care of his siblings and the family's business affairs.

Upon his return, he sought out as a spiritual director Father Nicolas Roland, a fellow canon at the cathedral in Reims. Following Roland's advice, De La Salle finished his studies at the University of Reims and, two months after the death of his father, was ordained as a subdeacon. A few weeks after this ordination, his older sister, along with his two-year-old brother, went to live with his maternal grandmother. With his other sister having entered the Canonesses of St. Augustine, the twenty-one-year-old De La Salle was left in charge of his three brothers who were aged thirteen, eight, and six. Several years of study and domestic responsibilities followed. Six years later, at the beginning of Lent in 1678, De La Salle had achieved a Licentiate in Sacred Theology, and on Holy Saturday, April 9, 1678, he was ordained to the priesthood by Charles-Maurice Le Tellier, the Archbishop of Reims. He had finally reached the goal that he had set out to obtain some eighteen years earlier but had done so in circumstances he could never have foreseen.

After his ordination, De La Salle no doubt saw before him a marginally successful career as a well-regarded cleric in the Diocese of Reims. But things were not to be that predictable. Within three weeks of his ordination, his spiritual director, Nicolas Roland, died while still fairly young, leaving De La Salle as one of the executors of his will. Among other things, the newly ordained twenty-seven-year-old was charged with completing Roland's negotiations for securing the legal recognition of the Sisters of the Holy Child Jesus, a religious order Roland had established for the education of poor girls. He did so, learning in the process which pastors, officials, and leading figures of Reims were the most helpful in such a project. De La Salle also advised these religious women on temporal matters and provided for their spiritual needs. His life was now busy with the daily five or six hours of prayer as canon of the cathedral, the priestly ministry of celebrating daily Eucharist and hearing confessions, and the hospitality he extended to various clerics at his house. Then he met Adrian Nyel.

Roland's congregation of teaching sisters had been modeled on the successful work of Father Nicolas Barrè and his religious sisters in Rouen, a work supported by the generosity of a Madame Maillefer, a relative by marriage to the De La Salle family. Adrian Nyel, an administrator at the General Hospice of Rouen (a place that provided various social services for the poor of the area, including education), had been recruiting young men with Barrè's help for the education of the poor boys of Rouen. In the middle of March in 1679, Adrian Nyel showed up at the door of the Sisters of the Holy Child Jesus in Reims with a message from Madame Maillefer that the education of poor boys in her hometown of Reims should be provided for, and he was there to do so. Providentially, De La Salle arrived at the same moment that Nyel did. They were introduced to each other and after some discussion the two of them spent a week at De La Salle's house working out strategies for accomplishing this new project. They consulted with experienced clerics and local pastors, many of whom De La Salle had been able to size up because of his work on behalf of Roland's Sisters. Eventually, it was determined that given the legal boundaries governing education at the time, the school should be a parish school under the authority of a local pastor.

Within just a few weeks, a school was established at the local parish of Saint Maurice and De La Salle thought that would be the end of his involvement in this project. Quite soon, however, another wealthy widow wanted to endow a similar Christian School for her own parish in Reims, but only if De La Salle was involved in the contract and promised to provide some supervision. Reluctantly, De La Salle gave his support. Nyel now had teachers for two schools housed at Saint Maurice, taxing the resources and goodwill of the pastor. De La Salle took another step toward greater involvement when he helped pay the pastor for the teachers' upkeep, but by December even that financial help wasn't enough. De La Salle decided that it was better to rent a house near his own for eighteen months, inviting Nyel and his teachers to be based there. Before long, Nyel also opened a Christian School in the parish in which their rented house was located. And while Nyel was great at establishing schools, he was not very good at inspiring, training, and supervising the teachers that he found to work in them.

De La Salle's response was to have the teachers join him for meals in his home, beginning at Easter of 1680, so that he might work more closely with them. He had promised to oversee the investment of those who had provided the funds for these schools, and this was the only way he could see himself fulfilling that promise. His involvement was still wholly external, yet his sense of responsibility led him, in his words, to try "to see to it that they carried out their duties in a religious and conscientious manner." In an interesting twist, at the same time as De La Salle was supporting the work of these barely literate "teachers," he was completing his own doctorate in theology at the University of Reims.

The following year saw the three initially successful schools suffer from Nyel's frequent absences as he explored the establishment of further schools, the lack of any uniform school policy or method, and the increasing need for discipline among the students and teachers. In response, De La Salle gave the teachers a retreat in his home during Holy Week of 1681, during which he tried to give them a spiritual vision of their work, instilling in them a sense of personal discipline. Nyel was again absent, negotiating the opening for yet another school. But when he returned, the change in the teachers was obvious to him, and he may have seen that the young De La Salle had a real future in this work of education.

De La Salle realized that without further input from himself, matters would quickly revert to the way they had been before. He consulted with Fr. Nicolas Barré in Paris, who knew both Roland and Nyel and was actively involved in the cause of education for the poor. The highly regarded priest quickly measured up both De La Salle and the situation and advised him to bring the teachers into his house and to live with them. Such a move would have clear consequences in terms of De La Salle's family (he was the guardian of his younger brothers), his place in society and the church (the mixing of social classes in this way was not done), and his future plans (any thought of ecclesiastical advancement would, at least, have to be put on hold). This would be a pivotal decision in his life. After he had prayed and consulted with others, De La Salle became convinced that this was the will of God for him, and he moved forward without further hesitation.

On June 24, 1681, when the lease on the rented house ran out, these simple teachers who were of a social class entirely removed from De La Salle's, moved into the house that De La Salle had lived in since the age of fourteen. When it became clear to his family that he would not change his mind, despite their interventions and protests, it was decided that one of his younger brothers would live with their older married sister, and the youngest would go to a boarding school. John Baptist's eighteen-year-old brother Jean-Louis, who would eventually become a priest himself, decided to stay with his brother and the schoolteachers.

Through the adoption of a uniform schedule for both house and school, the practice of common religious exercises and ascetical practices, and the inclusion of practical and consistent educational methods, De La Salle strove to slowly form this group of teachers into one that would have a common spirit and purpose. According to Dom Maillefer, one of his early biographers, De La Salle "was content to lead the teachers by the hand, so to speak, to let them see from their own experience and from his exhortations and example what was the best course to follow." While Adrian Nyel spent his time working on new foundations in cities outside of Reims, De La Salle now directed the teachers and the schools within Reims. From the one central house in the city, teachers left each morning and afternoon to staff the three schools, sharing their experiences upon their return and discussing successes and mistakes with De La Salle who listened and dispensed what advice he could.

The relationship between De La Salle and Adrian Nyel, who was thirty-eight years older than De La Salle, seems to have been generally amiable and mutually supportive but never truly complementary. Nyel had a passion and ability for starting schools. De La Salle acquired a passion for directing and establishing them as solid Christian Schools staffed by dedicated and religiously motivated teachers. At the end of the first six months of living together at De La Salle's house, Nyel left to establish Christian Schools in the town of nearby Rethel and didn't return to Reims for four years, establishing other schools staffed by teachers that he recruited. Some of these new schools also acquired teachers trained by De La Salle in Reims. The contrast between these teachers and Nyel's recruits, in terms of piety and discipline, was startling to those supporting the schools. It became clear to both De La Salle and Adrian Nyel that their gifts lay in different directions.

De La Salle was becoming involved more deeply at every turn. In June of 1682, he had to move from his family home because the house was lost at auction following a lawsuit brought on by his brother-in-law, Jean Maillefer. A number of schoolteachers, along with De La Salle's brother Jean-Louis, joined De La Salle when he moved to a rented double house on Rue Nueve in the poorer section of Reims, a house that would come to be known as the "cradle of the Institute." Besides changing houses, De La Salle changed social milieus. Instead of richly appointed spacious rooms, there would be cramped quarters. Instead of everyday servants, refined conversations, delicate aromas, and fine foods there would be no servants, simple conversation, questionable smells, and coarse food. At this new location, the men with De La Salle began to be called "Brothers" instead of "the schoolteachers who live with the priest De La Salle."

From the first, De La Salle was the superior of the group and, by request, their spiritual director. In a notable exception to most other religious communities of the time, nothing was introduced by authority. Instead, "he flattered them by giving them the satisfaction of being themselves the creators of their own vision and their own plans for making it a reality. In this way they became, in effect, their own legislators" (Aroz, 1980, p. 23). Within six months, however, the novelty had worn off and all but a few of the original group had left, something De La Salle didn't oppose once it became clear that the individuals weren't cut out for teaching or community life. New recruits arrived who were better disposed for the life De La Salle was proposing.

Yet the process of deeper involvement was far from over. Although both the schools and the Brothers' community life were apparently progressing well, the Brothers became confident enough to challenge De La Salle's security as compared to their

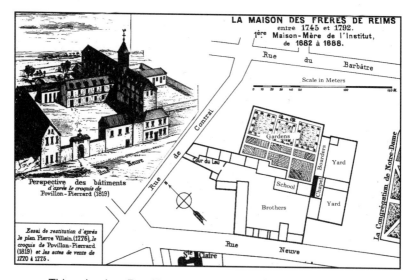

This school on Rue Neuve in Reims would become known as "the cradle of the Institute" because of its formative influence on De La Salle and the first Brothers.

own insecurity. Trusting in God might be a regular theme in De La Salle's talks to them, but the theme of his family fortune and position in society spoke more convincingly. "It is easy for you to talk," they told him.

> You have everything you need. You are a rich canon with a regular source of income and a guaranteed inheritance. You don't know what it is to have to do without. If our enterprise falls apart, you will survive and the collapse of our situation will not involve your own. But we are without property, without income, and we don't even have a marketable skill. Where will we go or what will we do if the schools fail and the people no longer want us? The only thing we will have left is our poverty and the only solution will be to go out and beg. (Salm, 1996, p. 38)

Here were words that struck home. The gradual conversion to the Gospel, which had begun with the encounter with Adrian Nyel was reaching evermore deeply into previously unchallenged dimensions of his life. De La Salle responded in the same way he would respond in all times of decision: by seeking God's will through prayer, fasting, consultation, reflection, openness to the immediate life around him, and by resolute but prudent action.

His response was as uncompromising as his developing character. In August of 1683, he resigned his canonry. When he wrote out for himself the reasons why he made this move, the last of the ten points listed typifies his approach to the discernment of God's will: "Since I no longer feel myself drawn to the vocation of a canon, it seems to me that this particular vocation has already left me long before I have abandoned it. This state in life is no longer for me. Although I entered it freely through an open door, it seems to me that today God is opening the door again so that I can leave it." (Salm, 1996, p. 39)

After losing the income from his benefice as canon of the Cathedral of Reims, his other financial assets remained to be dealt with. De La Salle resisted the idea of endowing the schools—the natural expectation—on anything less than God's Providence, praying that "If You endow them, they will be well endowed; if You do not endow them, they will stay without endowment." (Calcutt, 1993, p. 171) Instead, during the great winter famine of 1683–1684, De La Salle used his fortune to distribute food daily to all who were in need. W.J. Battersby, FSC, a later biographer of De La Salle, writes:

During the terrible winter and famine of 1684–1685,
De La Salle distributed his fortune to the poor and the needy by
giving out bread. Painting by Giovanni Gagliardi, 1901.

From all the surrounding countryside beggars flocked into the town in search of food, and the townsfolk themselves were driven to the extremity of misery by the scarcity and high cost of provisions. All he had to do, therefore, was to stand at the door of his house each day and distribute bread to those who wanted it. It soon became known that food was to be obtained for the asking and his house was besieged. At the same time he reserved a certain amount for the famished children in his schools." (Battersby, 1958, p. 65)

We can't say exactly how much De La Salle gave away. One modern estimate puts the amount at about 9,000 *livres,* with one *livre* worth roughly $50.00 in today's currency and an even higher relative value in the society of the time. By way of comparison, we do know that he kept enough to provide for himself a basic annual income of two hundred *livres,* the standard salary for teachers.

The Brothers themselves were amazed at De La Salle's reaction to their challenge, but they could hardly fault him for responding so conclusively. Yet now that all were reduced to poverty, their insecurity stood out all the more. De La Salle urged them to look about them and notice that while many rich merchants and well-to-do communities had been ruined, they who were without capital or revenue had never lacked the basic necessities. This reliance on Providence through poverty was something that he would maintain throughout his life, writing later on that the Brothers would survive only as long as they remained poor; they would lose the spirit of their state once they began to get used to comforts beyond what was needed to support life.

In 1685, the four schools Adrian Nyel had started in other towns were placed in De La Salle's care as the sixty-year-old Nyel decided, despite De La Salle's attempts to change his mind, to return to Rouen and the General Hospice from where he had started his educational ventures in Reims and beyond six years earlier. Nyel's energies and enthusiasm were on the decline, and when two years later he died of lung disease, De La Salle and the Brothers deeply mourned his death.

Now the entire community and all seven schools were in De La Salle's hands. As the teachers' public posture increased, their commitment consolidated with the adoption of a common habit, "a poor and modest habit" that caused more than a little ridicule and mockery over the years, and a name, "Brothers of the Christian Schools." At a general assembly of twelve of the principal Brothers, held in 1686, and after a spiritual retreat led by De La Salle, the habit and name were officially adopted. At the same time, it was decided that the drafting of a *Rule* would be deferred in order to learn from further experience. The assembled Brothers decided to take a private vow of obedience for three years, renewable annually, and they did so with De La Salle on Trinity Sunday, 1686. The next day they made a thirty-mile pilgrimage on foot to the shrine of Our Lady of Liesse where they renewed their vow of obedience and entrusted the future of the Institute to Mary.

The Brothers' sense of community and communal mission became ever stronger. Repeated requests to staff rural schools had to be denied since they had adopted the policy of never sending fewer than two Brothers to a given school, and pastors could hardly pay for the support of even one teacher. But the training of teachers for the rural schools could be accomplished. This was a work in which De La Salle would always remained interested. In 1687, he began to take in young men from the villages of the Diocese of Reims, chosen and sent by their parish priests for training as teachers. He housed the first group of twenty-five in a building adjacent to that occupied by the Brothers. De La Salle oversaw their formation as Christian educators, and these teachers-in-training shared many common activities with the Brothers. In one sense, the job was done too well. After a few of these groups from the outlying parishes had been trained, no further teachers were needed for the country schools, and that particular enterprise came to an end. Later, as we shall see, such training schools were established again as the need arose.

The following year, in 1687, after the Brothers' retreat preceding Trinity Sunday, De La Salle insisted that the Brothers elect one of their own as Superior. Reluctantly, the Brothers elected Br. Henri L'Heureux. De La Salle was the first to kneel and offer obedience to the new Superior. But once they heard of this development, diocesan officials reacted far less favorably, unable to accept or fathom this sort of submissive arrangement of a cleric to a Brother. Before long, with a direct order from Archbishop Le Tellier, De La Salle was persuaded to resume his place as head of the Society.

Within the five years that they had lived at Rue Nueve, the group had come together with a distinct sense of community, a common vision and unified method for their successful educational works, and an increasingly clear sense of identity and purpose. Two things are worth noting at this point. First, the community as yet had no official "letters patent" and hence enjoyed no legal status. The Brothers fell under the jurisdiction of the parish priest in all that concerned the school, although it appears that in the day-to-day running of the group, De La Salle and the Brothers made their decisions with a minimum amount of consultation. Second, De La Salle rarely "opened" a school. He was usually invited to take over a school situation that already existed but that was in desperate need of a new approach.

De La Salle shows the pastor of the parish of Saint Sulpice
in Paris through the school on Rue Princesse.
Painting by Giovanni Gagliardi, 1901.

DE LA SALLE'S STORY – THE MIDDLE YEARS

As the work of the Brothers became a successful religious and educational enterprise, it wasn't long before there were opportunities to spread beyond Reims and its environs. In February of 1688, De La Salle and two Brothers came to Saint Sulpice in Paris, the same parish and church where he had had his seminary training. The school there exemplified all that was wrong with education: no fixed class schedule, daily variations in school hours, students coming and going at will, no uniform prayer or religious instruction, excessive attention paid to the hosiery factory attached to the school for "training" the students, and no discipline. While not in charge of the school, the Brothers, through quietly changing what they could within their classrooms, soon made an impact. Within a few months, De La Salle was asked to completely take over the school, receiving the financial means to bring two additional Brothers from Reims. The changes in the school were immediate and dramatic: a fixed schedule of classes with daily catechism and prayer as a focal point, a fixed time of coming and going to school (the doors were locked at all other times), daily attendance at the parish Mass during the long noon break, and less emphasis on working in the hosiery factory.

When another parish school was opened by De La Salle in 1690, it was legally challenged by the Masters of the Little Schools, a group of private teachers whose rights were traditionally defended by the diocesan superintendent of schools, Claude Joly, who oversaw all 167 Parisian school districts. The Masters alleged that the school was accepting paying students despite its being a charity school. After an initial victory in the courts, their argument was dismissed on appeal, but the legal battles in Paris were just beginning. This conflict over the schools would be fought out in various forms and venues for the next sixteen years until 1706. Between the Masters of the Little Schools, the Guild of Writing Masters (a sort of union of scribes who also ran writing schools), and the parish-controlled charity schools, each teaching similar subjects in different ways to separate clientele, and each claiming singular privileges, it is little wonder that even the appropriate authorities of the day could scarcely determine their separate legitimate claims to teach certain subjects and certain groups.

Challenges came from other quarters as well. The two Brothers who had originally come to Paris with De La Salle didn't agree with his decisions (one of them departed as a result), half the community in Reims left the Society with the remaining eight Brothers thinly stretched among the seven schools of the Reims area, the pastor of Saint Sulpice became uncooperative and was ready to step in and take over, De La Salle and the Brothers in Paris became exhausted with all the work, morale was low all around, and Br. Henri L'Heureux in Reims on whom De La Salle had placed his hope for taking over the whole enterprise became ill and died. Although this last event really hurt him on a deeply

An engraving of the country house at Vaugirard that became known as the second "cradle of the Institute" where De La Salle lived from 1691 to 1698.

personal level, De La Salle looked for and found a Providential dimension to the tragedy. Br. Henri had been in training for the priesthood, since he had not been accepted by diocesan officials as Superior of the Brothers as a Brother. With his death, De La Salle discerned that the Society should consist of Brothers alone, and that its nonclerical aspect was part of its character.

He also found a property on the outskirts of Paris, in Vaugirard, that could become a source of renewal for all of the Brothers and a novitiate for new candidates. In 1691, he brought everyone there for an extended retreat under his direction. Many of the Brothers had had little in terms of religious formation prior to being put before a classroom full of students. When De La Salle realized that more time would be needed for some of them, he prolonged the retreat into the school year, arranging to replace these Brothers in their schools with the rural lay teachers he had trained in Reims. This time of retreat was so successful that such periods of religious renewal became a regular part of the Brothers' yearly program. Eventually, the religious and educational themes that were taken up at these retreats were consolidated in De La Salle's *Meditations for the Time of Retreat,* a pivotal text that brought together many elements of the Brothers' teaching vocation.

After the retreat, the Brothers were instructed to write De La Salle monthly, giving an account of their behavior and their interior dispositions. He faithfully replied to these confidential letters. For over twenty-five years, they were his only link with many of the Brothers. It was in this way that the fervor engendered by the retreat was maintained throughout the year. The letters both helped the Brothers reflect on their progress in their vocation and kept De La Salle informed as to the state of the Society. The letters read like a conversation, reflecting a familiar manner. De La Salle's responses were direct and precise, with little if any small talk. Few of the many thousands of letters that De La Salle wrote in this way have survived. The 110 letters to various Brothers that have survived provide one of the more straightforward glimpses we have into De La Salle's character.

De La Salle also addressed the uncertainties and difficulties that the young community was facing. Choosing two zealous men who seemed the most committed to the work, he proposed that they take with him a private vow to establish this Society no matter what might happen, even "if we were obliged to beg for alms and to live on bread alone." They did so on November 21, 1691, at Vaugirard. For many years, no one else knew of this vow, later called the "heroic vow" by the Brothers. Although it would be tested in many ways, this declaration of association provided a foundation of intentionality and commitment on which they could build. Perhaps of some significance is the fact that exactly fifty years earlier Jean-Jacques Olier and two companions had made a similar private vow at Vaugirard to establish the seminary of Saint Sulpice, a place which subsequently had such a great influence in De La Salle's own spiritual formation.

De La Salle would often teach in schools himself, especially if one of the Brothers became ill or if circumstances called for his involvement. Painting by Cesare Mariani, 1888.

De La Salle began composing a *Rule* for the Brothers in the spring of 1694. The draft of this text was submitted to the Brothers with the clear understanding that they would be the ones who would add or subtract items as they saw fit, and they would be the ones who would approve it. This rule of life arising out of the Brothers' common experience took shape throughout De La Salle's lifetime and came to completion only after the General Chapter of 1717. The daily schedule from the years in Reims was adopted in 1686 and was subsequently modified and developed in the light of the Brothers' experience. When the 1694 *Rule* was put together, De La Salle's choices were quite eclectic, as he drew from many sources and adapted what he found as he saw fit.

In considering the question of introducing perpetual or life vows, De La Salle and the senior Brothers he consulted proposed the taking of vows that were specifically directed to their mission of extending the reign of God through education. On June 6, 1694, Trinity Sunday, these twelve senior Brothers and De La Salle privately made perpetual vows of association to conduct the gratuitous schools, stability in the Society, and obedience. When on the following day De La Salle recommended that the Brothers elect one of their own as Superior, he was promptly and unanimously re-elected, several times, much to his consternation. After the Brothers pointed out that this was simply God's will, De La Salle ceased trying to change their minds but had them sign a declaration stating, among other things, that

> the present election will not have the force of a precedent for the future. Our intention is that after the said John Baptist de La Salle, and forever in the future, no one shall be received among us or chosen as Superior who is a priest, or who has received Holy Orders; and that we will not have or accept any Superior who has not associated himself with us, and has not made vows like us and like all those who will be associated with us in the future. . . . (Salm, 1996, p. 79)

The unique character of the Society as an independent, nonclerical, mission-based, communal educational ministry was becoming more and more clear to De La Salle, and he would do all he could to preserve and strengthen that charism.

Now De La Salle and the Brothers began to fortify their Society, strengthening the already flourishing schools and communities, and forming the young candidates asking to join their way of life. De La Salle focused more on writing various texts, both for the schools and for the Brothers. Their breadth and content was truly striking, as will be specified later, included everything from a student reading text on politeness and decorum to a detailed method for the Brothers' interior prayer life. During the next fifteen years, between 1694 and 1709, new schools were opened and closed, Brothers entered the Society and left, legal battles with the Writing Masters and the teachers of the Little Schools raged on, and little by little the identity that De La Salle had begun to form among the Brothers took hold.

Some of the highlights of those years include the following:

- The Brothers established a Sunday School for Parisian working men under the age of twenty who wished either to continue their education beyond the elementary level or to learn to read and write if they had never attended school. Two of De La Salle's most talented Brothers taught reading, writing, mathematics, draftsmanship, catechism, and art on Sunday afternoons at this "Christian Sunday Academy."

- Schools were established in Chartres where, in response to the bishop's concern, De La Salle wrote a defense for teaching students French instead of Latin. French was much more practical than teaching Latin. French is easier to learn, takes less time, is more useful, may be a vehicle for learning Latin, is a necessary tool for learning other things (including Christian doctrine). Besides the fact that Latin is of little use to working people, there's not enough time to master it in the Christian Schools, and those who do know only a little look foolish trying to use it.

- One of the "heroic vow" participants, Br. Gabriel Drolin, was sent to Rome with Brother Gérard (who was also his blood brother) to establish a school there.

When they arrived, they couldn't speak the language, had few contacts, and found that education for the poor was well provided for. Besides, Rome had a highly organized clerically dominated school system that showed little interest in any other model of education. Brother Gérard soon returned to France, but Brother Gabriel remained in Rome for twenty-six years, faithfully struggling to get a foothold in the ecclesiastical school system. He eventually received a license to teach in one of the papal schools and finally established his own school, although he never received a second Brother as De La Salle had so often promised in the letters that are preserved.

• Schools were established in other towns and cities, including Calais, Avignon, Marseilles, and Grenoble, each school adopting its own characteristics based on local needs and the likely employment prospects that students would face. At the same time, the pedagogy and methodology were uniform throughout, based on the experiences and lessons learned among the other Christian Schools.

• The school and community at Saint Sulpice in Paris went through several crises. The archbishop of Paris appointed a new ecclesiastical superior for the Brothers because of perceived disciplinary severity on a part of several Brother superiors. De La Salle accepted this change, but the Brothers would have none of it, and only by means of a compromise did they accept an occasional visit to the house by such a superior. Then, in 1706, the courts of the Parliament, the major judicial body in Paris, forbade De La Salle and the Brothers "to establish any community under the name of a training school for teachers in the primary schools, or anything similar" in Paris or its environs without the express permission of the diocesan superintendent of schools. The Brothers at the three schools in the parish of Saint Sulpice responded by closing their three schools abruptly and leaving Paris virtually overnight. It was only by the direct appeal of the pastor to De La Salle and through a judicious compromise with the authorities that the Brothers were persuaded to return.

- The Brothers came to take over the four charity schools in Rouen that Adrian Nyel had overseen prior to his involvement with De La Salle. For two years, De La Salle and five Brothers lived in the city's General Hospice, caring for its inhabitants as part of their contract and running the charity schools besides. In 1705, they moved to Saint Yon, an extensive property away from city noise with a manor house, spacious gardens, and a quiet environment. Here the novices were trained, the annual retreat was held, and three new ventures were begun: a boarding school for older boys who were destined for careers in commerce and industry, the first secondary school curriculum of its kind; a house of correction for delinquent children where students were strictly supervised outside of common classes with the other students; and a house of detention for those young men confined by the courts by *lettres de cachet*. The Brothers' success in transforming many of their charges outweighed the difficulties and challenges that these new ventures presented, and the income that St. Yon generated served to support the work elsewhere.

- All of these new foundations, along with the daily concerns that demanded his attention, eventually required De La Salle to place a Brother in Avignon in charge of all the schools in the south, and to have another Brother visit the schools in and around Reims—hence the term "Visitors" for today's provincial superiors. Thus was he able to maintain the spirit behind the principle of "together and by association" and complement the unity engendered through the annual retreats and monthly correspondence.

De La Salle's Story – The Later Years

Later in his life, when he was reflecting on the early years, De La Salle writes that if he had known all of the difficulties and challenges that lay ahead, he never would have started the enterprise in the first place. It was now, as he was nearing the age of sixty, and after more than twenty-five years of working with the Brothers, that some of the most difficult hardships came to the fore.

The Brothers throughout France suffered with the rest of the population as cold weather, crop failures, and the demands of the War of the Spanish Succession led to a great famine in 1709 with all of its attendant miseries. The novices were moved back to Paris for some years so that the Brothers in Rouen might concentrate on their own needs. Many religious orders went bankrupt or were decimated by disease and death, but the Brothers survived, De La Salle constantly urging them to trust in Providence.

This tremendous trust in Providence that De La Salle displayed was neither naive nor falsely pious. He had had too many experiences that confirmed God's continual care for him and for the ministry of Christian education. At the same time, De La Salle worked hard to step forward in the direction in which God's will seemed to be leading him. His administrative capabilities were as thorough as they were visionary. While himself practicing many penances and encouraging the austere lifestyle of the Brothers, he was also concerned about their well-being, insisting, for example, that the Brothers' houses include a courtyard or a garden where the Brothers could spend time recouping from the time spent in the classroom.

The reputation of the Christian Schools continued to lead to new foundations in places such as Versailles and elsewhere, even as legal and ecclesial challenges were constantly being met across France. But for De La Salle himself, it was one legal situation that was to precipitate his greatest personal challenge. This is a little complex, but it is worth knowing, since it illustrates several dimensions of De La Salle's character and his historical situation.

In 1707, a young well-to-do layman, Jean-Charles Clément, offered to use a substantial part of his allowance to begin a center for the training of country schoolmasters. Despite De La

Salle's initial hesitance in the face of both the young man's enthusiasm and the still binding court order forbidding him to open any kind of teacher training school within the jurisdiction of the superintendent in Paris, De La Salle held a project such as this close to his heart and eventually provided a substantial down payment in 1708 so that Clément could purchase a property for the training center in Saint Denis, just outside of the Paris jurisdiction. The school opened in 1709 and soon duplicated the success of the earlier teacher training schools that the Brothers had conducted.

Since Clément was legally a minor—under the age of twenty-five—the house had been bought for him by a lawyer, who held a receipt signed by Clément assuring De La Salle of reimbursement once Clément received the benefice of the wealthy abbey of Saint Calais, an imminent event. When that benefice became an actuality in 1710, Clément's attitude changed, and he refused either to pay back De La Salle or to pay the balance of the purchase price, although Clément insisted that he wanted the house for himself. The picture became more complicated as the original owner tried to get the house back and the lawyer attempted to resell the house to another buyer. Once the young man's father, a well-known physician, became involved, the situation became even worse.

In 1711, after a brief journey to the south of France to visit the Brothers' communities there, De La Salle returned to Paris to find that the Clément family, recently granted noble status by the king, would accept nothing less than his public condemnation in the courts as a criminal who had taken advantage of a minor to advance his own aims. Neither De La Salle's offer to forgive the debt nor the evidence of the original arrangement was sufficient to outweigh the fact that Clément had been a minor. The court's judgment was brought against De La Salle on May 31, 1712. Not only did he have to cancel the debt and reimburse Clément for the money Clément had spent in supporting the training center, De La Salle was criminally condemned for trying to extort promises of money and warned to never again enter into business negotiations with minors.

When De La Salle found out from his lawyer in January 1712 that the case against him was lost, that the house at St. Denis would be confiscated, that the school would be closed down, and that there was a warrant out for his arrest, he decided to make a hasty getaway. Giving his lawyers all relevant documents and a detailed memoir on the entire history of the situation, De La Salle left Paris to resume his tour of the south. When the final judgment against him came in May, he was visiting the Brothers in Marseilles and so outside their jurisdiction.

To the Brothers in the north, this was a definite crisis. To have De La Salle leave them at a time of many difficulties seemed to them to be an abandonment. In actual fact, De La Salle had left the relatively unknown Director of Novices, Brother Barthélemy, in charge and was doing what he thought best for the Brothers.

> Barthélemy wrote to all the communities, to say that M. de La Salle was in good health, that he had had to flee, that the place where he had gone was known, and that, according to the intention of their common father, they could write to him [Barthélemy] and he would do what he could to content them. He made clear he was only a substitute for their real Superior until he returned and not by personal right, and that he would try to govern according to his spirit. This clarified the position for most, and they accepted him on those conditions. It was a touchy thing for them for any Brother to try to take the place of the one they regarded as a saint and as their indispensable Founder. Yet it was time, and past time, for them to face up to having a Brother installed as Superior General before he died and also to relieve an aging man of the burden. (Calcutt, 1993, p. 518)

De La Salle's second journey to the south of France, beginning in February 1712, lasted more than two years. We don't know whether this extended separation from the Brothers in the north was due to the decrease of his influence and an active opposition against him on the part of some church authorities in Paris, along with the legal decision against him, or to a genuine desire to remove himself from the Brothers' struggles toward independence. From what we know about his time in the south of France, however, it appears that he maintained a vigorous interest in both the schools and the religious development of the Brothers and their vocation.

After a month's stay visiting the Brothers and notables in Avignon, where the schools had been successfully established since 1703, De La Salle resumed the tour of communities that he had begun a year earlier. Everywhere he went, Brothers, pastors, and bishops treated him with great hospitality and respect, leading De La Salle often to cut short his visits or to depart in secrecy so as to avoid the accolades and honors given to him. During these visits, he would encourage the Brothers in their vocation, urging them to remain faithful to their religious duties. When supporters requested that individual Brothers be permanently assigned to their schools, he would explain the nature of the Society and the importance of the Society's autonomy despite its lack of canonical or legal status. Brothers must be able to be sent wherever they will be able to do the most good.

De La Salle tried to establish a novitiate in Marseilles, but this was not to be. Jansenism was too firmly established in the area. Also, the people could not see training candidates for work elsewhere in France, and even the Brothers' communities themselves resisted his efforts at reforming them from the rather easy lifestyle they had adopted.

Believing it best that he leave them to work things out for themselves, he quietly left Marseilles, climbing a steep thirty miles to the sacred grotto of Sainte Baume, famous as the supposed last habitation of Mary Magdalene. Here he sought God's will in solitude and prayer, as rumors circulated that De La Salle was about to leave the Society to the designs of Providence and retire to a remote parish in order to work for the conversion of hardened sinners. After spending some time at Sainte Baume, followed by forty days of retreat at the nearby monastery of Saint Maximin, he traveled to the community at Mende, where the Brothers had also cultivated an easy lifestyle. De La Salle couldn't budge them an inch and was further chagrined to find that the community couldn't (or wouldn't) accommodate him in the Brothers' house. For two months, he stayed first with the Capuchins and then with

Mlle. Lescure, the founder of the Ladies of the Christian Union, whom he aided in composing a rule for her teaching institute.

De La Salle became less and less convinced that he should maintain direction of the Brothers. The Brothers in Paris seemed fine without him, and those in and around Marseilles were little influenced by his direction. When the former director of the novitiate he had tried to establish in Marseilles, Brother Timothy, sought him out at Mlle. Lescure's home to report an empty novitiate and to request a new assignment, De La Salle's response was: "Why do you come to me with all of this? Don't you know that I am not competent to give orders to others? Are you not aware that there are many Brothers who no longer want to have anything to do with me? They say they no longer want me as their Superior. And they are right. I am really incapable of that any more." (Salm, 1996, p. 158) But he was persuaded by Brother Timothy that he was still wanted and needed.

In August 1713, De La Salle traveled to the Brothers' community in Grenoble, and here he was well received. Choosing an isolated cubicle in the recess of a tower, he remained in solitude and prayer for several months and worked on his writings. When he sent the Brother who was in charge of the school and the community north to obtain more information about the Brothers' situation there, De La Salle became fully involved in the school, teaching classes and regularly leading the children to the nearby church to celebrate Mass for them. The fervor of his piety made a great impression on the people of Grenoble, and he is still esteemed there today. But the harsh winter took its toll on his health and new attacks of rheumatism again threatened his life. The whole city offered prayers for his recovery.

Resolving to make another spiritual retreat, he went to a hermitage near Grenoble called Parménie. This hermitage had recently been built on the ruins of a medieval monastery. At this retreat center established by a devout and pious visionary named Sister Louise, De La Salle initially stayed fifteen days, spending time in conversation with her and subsequently corresponding with her. Some think that he seriously considered retiring at Parménie, perhaps as the resident spiritual director. But Sister Louise told him that his work with the Brothers was not yet done.

It was while De La Salle was in Grenoble that he received a letter, dated April 1, 1714, from the Directors and the principal Brothers of the Paris region. The Brothers there had been trying to contact him for a long time, but their letters had either never been delivered or had never been answered by De La Salle. The situation in Paris had become quite difficult due to the increasing influence of the Sulpician pastors in the Society's internal affairs and due to the need for guidance in many administrative matters that required a clear central authority. In this letter, these Brothers in effect ordered De La Salle to return by virtue of his vow of obedience to the body of the Society and to again take up its general government.

> Reverend and our very dear Father. We, the leading Brothers of the Christian Schools, having in view the greater glory of God, the greater good of the Church and of our Society, acknowledge that it is of extreme consequence that you should resume the care and the general conduct of the holy work of God which is also yours,

The retreat location in Parménie where De La Salle encountered Sister Louise and came to find that his work with the Brothers was not yet done.

since it has pleased the Lord to make use of you to found it and to guide it for so long.

Everyone is convinced that God gave you and still gives you the grace and the talents necessary to govern well this new Society, which is of such great usefulness to the Church, and we bear you the testimony in all justice that you have always led it with much success and edification.

And so, Monsieur, we beg you very humbly and we command you in the name of and on behalf of the body of the Society to which you have promised obedience, to take care immediately of the general government of our Society. (Bannon, 1988, p. 185)

On August 10, 1714, after stopping at various communities along the way, De La Salle arrived back in Paris with the words: "Well, here I am. What do you want of me?"

Instead of taking over the day-to-day affairs of the Society, he let it be known that he would resume his sacramental ministry only, giving advice where needed or asked for, but that Brother Barthèlemy would have to run the Society with the help of the senior Brothers.

Gradually, De La Salle's influence began to stabilize and to solve many of the administrative problems that had developed over the last few years. After a year in Paris, De La Salle had Brother Barthélemy and the few novices that remained return to Saint Yon in Rouen, coming there himself a month later. While the new Archbishop of Rouen was less supportive than his predecessor, the parish priests sought De La Salle out for advice on dealing with hardened sinners, and he found himself in continual demand as confessor and spiritual director.

At Saint Yon, De La Salle began to work toward providing for the Society's future stability. His austerities, extensive travel, and recurring illnesses (he was ill for ten months at Saint Yon) made him and the Brothers realize that they needed an elected successor who would carry on the work that De La Salle had begun. The clearest choice was Brother Barthélemy who had held the Society together during De La Salle's absence in the south and who now took care of the administrative details.

Toward the end of 1716, with De La Salle now sixty-five years old, Brother Barthélemy was sent to visit all the houses of the Brothers in preparation for a General Assembly the following year. He did so, gathering the Brothers' signatures as they agreed to the General Assembly. This document with the signatures of the Brothers in the communities of that time has proven to be a valuable source of information, listing all of the early communities and their members. There were at the time twenty-three communities with ninety-nine Brothers who signed the document, not including De La Salle, Br. Barthélemy, and Br. Gabriel Drolin in Rome.

Sixteen delegates, all Directors of the various houses, gathered on May 16, 1717, and elected Brother Barthélemy as the

On the left, De La Salle as a young 18-year-old Reims cathedral canon. On the right, De La Salle's features at the time of his death fifty years later.

new Superior. The *Common Rule* of the Brothers was then discussed. Time constraints and the multitude of details to be considered led to the decision that De La Salle should prepare a revised version of the *Rule* based on the Assembly's discussions. The next year, De La Salle completed this revision, adding, among other things, a long paragraph insisting on the central importance of the Spirit of Faith as a fundamental attitude in the mission of the Institute and a prescription for the Brothers to read the New Testament daily, "looking upon it as their first and principal rule." This *Rule* guided the Institute from 1718 until 1967 when it was fully revised according to the mandates of Vatican Council II.

After the election of Brother Barthélemy, De La Salle moved more and more into the background, referring all requests for advice or permission to the new Superior. When in October 1717, De La Salle had to go to Paris in order to accept a legacy left to him by the lawyer involved in the Clément affair—funds that, providentially, enabled the purchase of the Saint Yon property in Rouen—he stayed in seclusion at the Seminary of Saint Nicolas du Chardonnet for five months. At this center for clerical renewal and reform, he would not interfere with Brother Barthélemy's new role and would be able to avoid the honors and deferences given him by the Brothers. As was the case everywhere he went, his presence at the seminary made a profound impression on the priests and seminarians there.

Upon returning to Saint Yon, De La Salle's greatest satisfaction came from training the novices in how to engage in extensive periods of interior prayer. He wrote a treatise on prayer and collected together the various meditations he had been writing over the years for the Brothers' use. His sacramental ministry included the care of the Brothers, the boarding students, and the inmates of the house of detention, taking particular interest in winning over the hardened adults who were in residence there.

De La Salle became more and more ill in 1719. His rheumatism became chronic and attacks of asthma increased. His head sustained several injuries due to accidents, resulting in continual severe headaches that prevented him from reading and writing. He was gradually confined to bed, too weak to practice his sacramental ministry, with the exception of the Feast of Saint Joseph, the special patron and protector of the Society, when he recovered enough to celebrate Mass for the Brothers. He received communion on Wednesday of Holy Week and he was given the sacrament of the sick (called "last anointing" at the time) on Holy Thursday. Toward evening on that day he was able to give the Brothers some final advice, urging them to avoid too familiar dealings with people of the world because this would lead to disenchantment and the loss of one's vocation. At about midnight, in response to Brother Barthélemy's question as to whether he accepted his sufferings, De La Salle replied with his last words: "Oui, j'adore en toutes choses la conduite de Dieu à mon égard."

("Yes, I adore in all things the conduct of God in my regard." *or* "Yes, I adore God guiding me in all the events of my life.")

At four o'clock in the morning on Good Friday, De La Salle made an effort to rise from his bed as if to greet someone, then joined his hands, raised his eyes to heaven, and died. He was buried on Holy Saturday in a side chapel of the local parish church, Saint Sever. Since it was Holy Week, the more solemn funeral rituals were delayed until the following week. Throughout Rouen, and soon throughout the Society, word spread that "the Saint is dead." But the extension of his life, work, and influence was just beginning.

An engraving by Trichon from a drawing by Farnier of De La Salle's funeral procession on Holy Saturday afternoon, April 8, 1719.

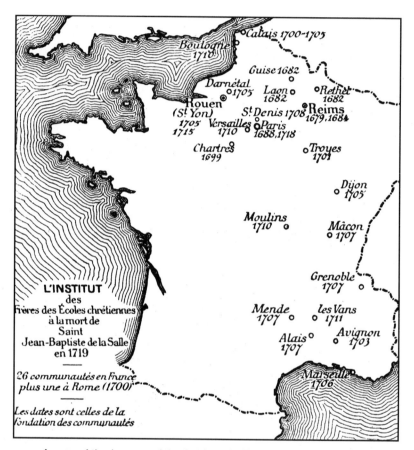

A map of the houses of the Institute in France at the time of the death of the Founder. Today's best estimate is that when De La Salle died in 1719, there were 23 Brothers' communities, or houses, that served 37 educational institutions out of a total of almost 60 schools that De La Salle and the Brothers had taken on or established during his lifetime.

♥

3

De La Salle's Educational Vision

When arriving at a new Lasallian institution, it takes only a little while to realize that this is indeed a place where Saint John Baptist de La Salle's vision and charism are lived out. Exactly what that looks like is harder to specify. It involves an entire spectrum of observations, expectations, experiences, and symbols. The recognition of a particular identity is more like the kind of knowledge that allows us to never forget a face. When we have to describe a particular face, we're stumped. But show it to us in a lineup and more than likely we'll pick it right out. Similarly, when we have to describe what a Lasallian institution looks like, we're stumped. But take us around to five different schools, one of which is Lasallian, and more than likely we'll pick it right out, given our previous experience of Lasallian schools.

What we *can* do when describing a person, beyond trying to describe the face, is to describe his or her personality. This may include facts about the person, statements the person has made, viewpoints he or she has expressed, and things that the person has done. On a deeper level it consists of the telling of stories—things the person has done, situations the person has transformed, quirks the person has taken on, and so on. Such stories begin to fill in the details of a picture that we can carry with us.

Similarly, in trying to describe what it means to be Lasallian we are trying to describe the "personality" of this particular educational heritage. The educational facts, viewpoints, and activities of this heritage will be presented in this chapter. The stories, of course, are the best part, but this is not the place to present them. These stories are the ones you carry with you based on your experience with the Lasallian tradition. Sharing these with one another is the very important "missing chapter" of this book. Such stories flesh out the educational vision and practice that De La Salle presents in his writings. As such, they give Lasallian "personality" its life.

There is a vast body of writings from which to choose the educational facts, viewpoints, and activities that identify the Lasallian tradition. The recently published French volume of De La Salle's complete writings is almost sixteen hundred pages. De La Salle's writings were almost always practical works, written to fulfill particular needs in the schools or in the Brothers community. His works for the schools include *The Conduct of Christian Schools* (in manuscript form until 1720), *Exercises of Piety for the Use of the Christian Schools* (1696), *Instructions and Prayers for Holy Mass* (1698), *Teaching French Syllables* (1698), *How to Go to Confession* (1698), *Prayers for Confession and Communion* (1698?), *The Rules of Christian Politeness and Civility* (1702), *Spiritual Canticles for the Use of the Christian Schools* (1703), *The Duties of a Christian,* or *The Catechism of the Brothers of the Christian Schools* (1703), a large abridgment and a small abridgment of *The Duties* (1703), *Christian Public Worship* (volume III of *The Duties;* 1703), *The Duties of a Christian* in continuous text of three volumes (1703), and *David's Psalter and the Office of Our Lady* (1706). His works for the Brothers' community include *The Common Rule of the Brothers of the Christian Schools* (1694, 1705, and 1718), *The Collection of Short Treatises for the Use of the Brothers of the Christian Schools* (1705; printed in 1711), *The Rule of the Brother Director of a House of the Institute, Meditations for All the Sundays of the Year and for the Principal Feasts of the Year, Meditations for the Time of the Retreat,* and *Explanation of the Method of Interior Prayer* (these latter ones were published after his death).

The writings of De La Salle are listed here just to give an idea of the breadth of his interests and the practical nature of his efforts. He was a man for whom the work of the schools and the ministry of the Brothers in the schools were primary. There are no treatises of educational philosophy to look at, no armchair reflections on educational methodology to critique, and no empty pious exhortations to repeat. The Brothers and his own experience would call him to task the minute he tried to do any of these, as they had challenged him years earlier concerning his canonry and his personal fortune. De La Salle instead wrote for what was needed as it was needed. Was there no book of French syllables when he decided that students should learn French before learning Latin? He wrote one, which, by the way, was credited much later as helping to establish a consistent way of speaking French throughout France. Was there no reading book in French suitable to the age group of the Brothers' students? He wrote one on good manners, so that students would learn something worthwhile from what they read. Was there no book of songs that students could sing as part of their religious training? He wrote one, taking popular tunes and writing lyrics on religious themes. Was there no resource for the Brothers' daily personal prayer times, one that could focus specifically on educational ministry? He wrote one, and in the process included a set of meditations for the time of retreat that are perhaps the best thing written yet on what it means to be an educator in the church. Was there no systematic presentation for either running schools or for presenting the Catholic faith to youngsters? He wrote one book for each, a handbook on how to run good schools (written over a period of twenty years in collaboration with the Brothers) and a comprehensive catechism on what it takes to be a good Christian. The list goes on. The point is that each book De La Salle wrote was written for a practical reason and based on the real experiences of real teachers and real students in real schools. It is from this rich set of resources that we must look for the Lasallian educational vision and practice.

The reader will be able to see by now that such a task is impossible to do comprehensively. Therefore, only highlights will be presented. These will come primarily from two sources: the *Meditations for All the Sundays of the Year and for the Principal Feasts of the Year, Meditations for the Time of the Retreat (hereafter, Meditations)* that he wrote on educational themes, and *The Conduct of*

Christian Schools (hereafter, *Conduct*), a handbook that he wrote with the input of the Brothers.

The *Meditations* were written as seeds of reflection, drawn out considerations of various aspects of the Brothers' lives. They include both specific religious themes and specific educational ones. Overall, it is the religious viewpoint that remains primary. The *Conduct* was written as a handbook for the running of schools; it contains pragmatic considerations of various aspects of the Brothers' lives. It also includes both specific religious themes and specific educational ones. Overall, it is the educational viewpoint that remains primary here. Where the *Meditations* will urge the Brothers to act as fathers and mothers to their pupils or to work as ambassadors of Christ, the *Conduct* supplies the organizational structure and concrete steps whereby one does so. Where the *Conduct* provides detailed guidelines for student correction, the *Meditations* provides the rationale for the kind of correction being suggested. These two works together make up one interwoven representation which intimately linked all aspects of the educational reality envisioned by De La Salle, a vision based on the seamless dialectical relationship between faith and zeal.

THE KEY RELATIONSHIP BETWEEN FAITH AND ZEAL

The major themes that came to be identified with Lasallian vision and practice center around the deep life of faith among the Brothers and the tremendous zeal they showed in establishing and operating the Christian Schools.

> De La Salle's paramount concern was to bring his Brothers to realize that in their work as educators, it is "the work of God" which is involved; God has chosen them to collaborate in the history of salvation, in a spirit of faith and zeal. They must, therefore, live as men of the interior, dwelling and working in the presence of God and abandoning themselves entirely to His guidance. (Hermans and Sauvage, in Mann, 1974, p. 32)

De La Salle's educational vision may be tightly summarized as an integration of faith and zeal through the transforming, dynamic presence of the spirit of Jesus Christ, the Holy Spirit, in a teaching community of chosen individuals. The spirit of faith consists in looking on all things with the eyes of faith, doing all things in view of God, and attributing all things to God. This faith leads one to dwell continually in the presence of God. The spirit of zeal seeks the salvation of students through prayer, instruction, vigilance, and good example, according to the Christian spirit and as found in the Gospel. This faith and this zeal find their dynamic integration in the Holy Spirit, who leads, animates, and transforms the teaching ministry into one of hope, love, and power. The spirit of Jesus Christ, encountered in prayer and in the classroom, is the living presence through whom, by whom, and in whom the work of education proceeds. The Brothers' spiritual quest, experienced within their ministry, is their continual conversion toward the person of Jesus Christ, both in his exterior actions and in his interior dispositions, which conversion is affected through a detachment from all that might bind, an awareness of God's constant presence, an abandonment to God's will, and a sublime confidence in God's providence.

De La Salle's wide scope of writings include the Brothers' Rule, meditations on teaching, a book on politeness, catechisms, prayer books, school textbooks, a handbook for teachers and administrators, song-texts, and others. Engraving by Chapon of a painting by Muller.

Three major dimensions of the central spirit of faith and zeal deserve particular consideration: (1) the nature of faith and of zeal, (2) the integration of faith and zeal, and (3) the context of faith and zeal. It is the following juxtaposition of these two terms, *faith* and *zeal,* that ultimately characterizes the nature of Lasallian vision and practice:

First, the nature and scope of faith and zeal are clearly spelled out at the very beginning of the 1705 *Rule.*

> The Spirit of this Institute is first a Spirit of faith which should lead those who belong to it to look upon nothing except with the eyes of faith, to do nothing except in view of God and to attribute all to God. . . . Secondly, the Spirit of this Institute consists in an ardent zeal for the instruction of children and for bringing them up in the fear of God, inducing them to preserve their innocence if they have not lost it, and inspiring them with a great aversion and horror for sin and whatever might cause them to lose purity. In order to enter into this Spirit, the Brothers of the Society shall strive by prayer, instruction, and by their vigilance and good conduct in school to procure the salvation of the children confided to their care, bringing them up in piety and in a true Christian spirit, that is, according to the rules and maxims of the Gospels. . . .

From the innocent faith of his relatively secure youth, through the searching faith of his increasing commitment to the work of the Brothers, to the deeply aged faith of his later years, this relentless movement of faithful adherence to God's call gradually became a familiar aspect of his daily existence. As the demands of faith influenced more and more of De La Salle's commitments, he came to see that faith itself was the source and means for effective Christian education. It is by faith that his followers entered into the dispositions of Jesus Christ within the tasks of daily life, and specifically within the work of Christian education. Faith, he writes, leads us "efficaciously to the knowledge, love, and imitation of Christ, and to union with him. . . . " It motivates us toward action, finding expression in zeal.

Second, this spirit of faith and zeal is a single spirit that consists of two interrelated parts. Faith and zeal are intimately bound up with each other, zeal emerging from an active faith and faith being formed by the fruits of zeal. Love for God is manifest through the zeal by which the activity of salvation becomes incarnate in the activities of the classroom. De La Salle makes no distinction between the two in the effective living out of the teaching vocation. "Do not distinguish between the duties of your state and what pertains to your salvation and perfection. Rest assured that you will never effect your salvation more certainly and that you will never acquire greater perfection than by fulfilling well the duties of your state, provided you do so with a view to accomplishing the will of God."

This seamless dialectical integration of faith and zeal is evident throughout De La Salle's life, becoming a central theme for both his own developing vocation as Founder and for the lives and vocations of those whom he shaped. The community and school were not separate realities, but were rather two dimensions of the same reality. "The work called for laymen working together in the spirit of faith or the daily pursuit of living by the Gospel, a faith that became activated as zeal in the presence of the needs of the children. In time, he and his Brothers had evolved a way of life perfectly fitting this vocation" (Calcutt, 1993, p. 261). Teaching no longer needed to be considered as something without honor, a profession that only served to provide a meager living. Teaching need not only be a means for exercising charity or for training new clerics. Motivated by faith and directed through zeal, teaching could become a way whereby the Gospel was practiced and preached, a worthy end in itself. "It is the first time in the history of religious communities that the teaching ministry is set out as being by itself a way of Christian perfection" (Calcutt, 1993, p. 278).

The integration of faith and zeal that became a hallmark of the Lasallian heritage also stands out in De La Salle's own life. De La Salle maintained in his letters that he never made the first move in any enterprise. He let God make the first move, and then he responded accordingly. As his faith knew no bounds, so also his zeal knew no bounds. If a city or town desired to have a Christian School, he would do all that he could to provide the Brothers to establish one. If the faith-life of his followers needed consistent direction, he would write to each one monthly and establish yearly retreats for them. If it seemed better to remove himself from a place in order to let the work succeed, he would do so, having faith in God's designs for both himself and for the work he had begun.

Faith and zeal were two aspects of the same commitment, two dimensions of the same experience. One without the other would have been an empty shell. Without zeal, faith had no substance, and without faith, zeal had no purpose. Faith and zeal more than complemented each other; they brought both to life. With zeal, faith found expression, and with faith, zeal found direction. In De La Salle, both came to fruition in the ministry of teaching and the work of education.

Third, faith and zeal do not operate in a vacuum. They are part of a spirituality that maintains a particular posture toward God and toward God's way of being in the world. De La Salle and his Brothers directed their faith and their zeal toward the work of education, but their goal was nothing less than the salvation of their students and themselves, a salvation brought about by following God's will.

God's will is encountered at every moment of one's life through the presence and activity of the Holy Spirit. Faith and zeal bring about the work of a new creation by evoking the "new law [given at Pentecost], and it is the law of grace and love." Through prayer, one abandons oneself entirely to the Holy Spirit's movement within the soul, because only the Holy Spirit is able to move "spiritually" those being taught.

God's designs are fully and constantly directed toward our good. God wills that all be saved, and it is for this purpose that God had called the Brothers to their ministry. Faith and zeal operate in a context that is permeated by the loving presence of God, a presence that is recalled at the beginning of each common activity within the community, and a presence whose recollection begins each prayer in the school and punctuates the classroom day at each hour.

De La Salle's encounter with God's loving presence becomes particularly focused in his absolute dependence on Divine Providence. God's providential care, manifest in all people and all events, large or small, is the ground out of which faith and zeal spring. The story of De La Salle's life illustrates the depth of commitment he made to that abandonment to Providence, and his writings are suffused with recommendations in the same vein; for example, " . . . the more fully we abandon ourselves to the care of Providence, the more attentive God is not to let us want for anything." De La Salle formed his Brothers toward the conviction that it was God who accomplished the work of Christian education through them and it was God who would give them all they needed for the task, as long as they abandoned themselves entirely to God. His prevailing sentiment was, "Lord, the work is Yours."

An engraving by Armand Gautier entitled "The Thursday Walk," 1853, that depicts the Brothers on a walk during their recreation time.

ELEMENTS OF DE LA SALLE'S VISION AND PRACTICE

De La Salle's reflections and the Lasallian practices that followed will be considered under five areas: (1) the Brother or Lasallian educator, (2) the student, (3) the teacher–student relationship, (4) the activity of teaching, and (5) the school. In each of these areas, allowance must be made for the fact that these sentiments come from seventeenth-century France. It will be the task of the next chapter to look at them in terms of contemporary life.

Without apology, most of the writings that De La Salle produced were intended for the Brothers and the Brothers alone. His *Meditations for the Time of Retreat* does include in its longer French title a reference to others who are involved in teaching, (Méditations pour le Temps de la Retraite à l'usage de toutes les Personnes qui s'emploient à l'éducation de la jeunesse; et particulièrement pour la Retraite que font les Frères des Ecoles chrétiennes pendant les Vacances) but generally speaking De La Salle focused on the Brothers. Yet it was also clearly De La Salle's conviction, demonstrated by his constant interest in the training of other teachers, that his educational vision and practice arose from the Gospel and, as such, is universally accessible to all those who take teaching as their vocation and as their ministry. This is a perspective that the worldwide Lasallian community takes to heart now more than ever.

In order to make the point more concretely, I will be changing the word *Brother* to the term *Lasallian educator* each time it occurs in the text that follows. This is neither to change the expectations that are made of the Brothers in their religious consecration through the mission of education, nor to make unfair expectations of colleagues in our schools who have little inclination toward becoming "pseudo Brothers." It is, rather, an attempt to recognize the fact that when De La Salle and the early Brothers focused on education, they did so with a vision and a set of practices that invite universal appreciation by all who take the Gospel seriously within an educational setting. In the sections that follow, all the text within quotation marks are words, phrases or statements from De La Salle's published writings.

THE LASALLIAN EDUCATOR

The Lasallian Educator's Calling

For De La Salle, the vocation of a teacher is both a great gift and a great responsibility. "It is a great gift of God, this grace he has given you to be entrusted with the instruction of children, to announce the Gospel to them and to bring them up in the spirit of religion. . . . " In his meditations, he urges Lasallian educators to be grateful for the "good fortune" of being able to "procure the sanctification of others."

Just as Jesus Christ entrusted his Apostles with spreading the Gospel, Lasallian educators are sent by Jesus Christ and commissioned by the church to do the same. "You must look upon yourselves as persons to whom the deposit of the faith has been confided, so that you may pass it on to them. This is the treasure God has placed in your hands, and of which he has constituted you the manager."

The vocation of the Lasallian educator is one of hidden glory, without immediate reward or universal appeal. "It is indeed a great honor for you to instruct your disciples about the truths of the Gospel solely for the love of God." They have been chosen to do a work that is esteemed and honored only by those who have a truly Christian spirit.

What a Lasallian Educator Is to Be

De La Salle utilizes a large number of images from the Scriptures, popular piety, and daily life in describing the kind of educator that he envisions. As can be seen in the following passage, his key image of a Lasallian educator is centered on the person of Jesus himself:

> Since you are ambassadors and ministers of Jesus Christ in the work that you do, you must act as representing Jesus Christ himself. He wants your disciples to see him in you and receive your instructions as if he were giving them to them [2 Corinthians 5:20]. They must be convinced that the truth of Jesus Christ comes from your

mouth, that it is only in his name that you teach, and that he has given you authority over them.

Yet it is not enough for the Lasallian educator to "resemble Jesus Christ only in his guidance and in his conversion of souls." One must also enter into his purposes and his goals. Otherwise, the teacher bears the name of "Christian" or "minister of Jesus Christ" in vain. The challenge is to live up to the teaching vocation that has been given to the one so called.

Christian educators, as "God's voice," are the means by which God spreads the Gospel. "Jesus Christ has chosen you among so many others *to be his cooperators* [1 Corinthians 3:9] in the salvation of souls." They have taken on the duties of the Apostles. Like Saint John the Baptist, they are precursors of Jesus Christ, preparing the way for his coming. In their work, Lasallian educators "are like good architects who give all possible care and attention to lay the foundation of religion and Christian piety in the hearts of these children [1 Corinthians 3:10], a great number of whom would otherwise be abandoned."

Lasallian educators must also look upon themselves as sharing in the ministry of the guardian angels, enlightening minds with the light needed to know God's will and to achieve salvation, and inspiring their students, procuring for them "the means to do the good that is proper to them." Lasallian educators are called to be "good guides and visible angels," guiding their students on the road to heaven.

What a Lasallian Educator Is to Have

Lasallian educators are to have a combination of dedication and goodness, courage and faith, a "very ardent zeal" matched with a "generous disposition," a combination of concern and vigilance. "The more virtue and perfection your state demands of you, the more strength and generosity you will need to achieve this," such strength being found particularly in the Eucharist.

The Lasallian educator "should live and be guided only according to the spirit and the light of faith; it is only the Spirit of God who can give you this disposition." "A simple faith in the mysteries would be enough for yourself, but it is not enough for you to be able to give them what they need." In order to give the "spirit of Christianity . . . to others you have to possess it well yourself."

In order to acquire such a spirit, one must seek out "the friendship of Jesus" so that he "may love you tenderly and take pleasure in being with you." As the branch draws its sap and strength from the vine, "you will be true and effective only insofar as Jesus Christ gives [your work] his blessing and as you remain united with him."

The Lasallian educators' way of life should be a model for their students "because they ought to find in you the virtues they should practice." In the *Collection of Short Treatises,* these virtues are specified under the heading of "The Twelve Virtues of a Good Teacher" as seriousness, silence, humility, prudence, wisdom, patience, reserve, meekness, zeal, vigilance, piety, and generosity.

What a Lasallian Educator Is to Do

The content of Christian instruction comes from God and proceeds through the teacher to the student by virtue of God's action within that teacher. The task of the teacher begins with the acquisition of that which is necessary for an effective ministry.

Since God realizes that the Lasallian educator has "neither enough virtue nor enough ability" to give students all that is necessary, one must ask God for these graces "frequently, fervently, and insistently." Following the teaching of Saint Augustine, the Lasallian educator must first learn those things that are to be taught and must first practice those things that are to be exhorted. "Ask God, then, for what you lack, and to give you what you need in full measure, namely, the Christian spirit and deep religious convictions." One should "not be content . . . to read and to learn from others what you must teach your students." One must ask God "to impress all these truths . . . firmly on yourselves."

The process of Christian instruction depends as much on example as on any other component. The teacher must model what is being taught. "Preach by your example, and practice before [the students'] eyes what you wish to convince them to believe and do." The truth of the Gospel will be made "effective for others only in so far as it has first produced its effect in you." Instruction supported by example is one of the chief characteristics of the Lasallian educator's zeal. Without it, one's zeal "would not go very far and would not have much result or success." Zeal must, as a model to the students, be realized within one's behavior.

The foundation of Christian instruction consists in the Lasallian educator's active prayer life. "Strive to know God so well through reading and interior prayer that you may be able to make him known to others, and make him loved by all those to whom you have made him known." "By prayer you will draw upon yourselves the grace of God that you need to do this work." Prayer obtains all that one needs for effective teaching, drawing "upon yourself the light you must have to know how to form Jesus Christ in the hearts of the children entrusted to your guidance."

De La Salle tells his teachers to turn to God before, during, and after the exercise of one's ministry. "You must constantly represent the needs of your disciples to Jesus Christ, explaining to him the difficulties you experience in guiding them." Prayer "gives a holy power" to one's words, making the Lasallian educator able to effectively penetrate the depths of their students' hearts. The more prayer is practiced, "the more God will help you find the skill to touch their hearts."

THE STUDENT

The Identity of Students

Throughout his meditations, De La Salle rarely uses the term *students (élève);* most often he uses the term *disciple* (seventy-one times as compared to twenty for élève). While the term *disciple* referred directly to the mission or vocation of the Lasallian educator to make these students disciples of Jesus Christ, it also informed the relationship between teacher and pupil. Popular education in the seventeenth-century being what it was, the relationship between teacher and pupil was hardly ever more than a commercial one at best. By describing them as disciples, De La Salle not only established an essentially religious component in the relationship between teacher and pupil but also introduced an element of responsibility that gave students a central place in the educational enterprise.

Disciples are not taught in the ordinary sense. The concern is not simply for the passing on of knowledge. Rather, the students are an extension of the teacher, taking on the teacher's convictions, commitments, and practices—in a word, taking on the teacher's spirituality. A teacher with disciples has a personal interest in them since they represent all that the teacher imparts to them. By calling students *disciples,* De La Salle from the start indicates the kind of Christian relationship that he expects between teacher and pupil in a school.

De La Salle also highlights the value that students have by articulating the nature of their religious identity. "Look upon the children God has entrusted to you as the children of God himself." In that respect they deserve greater consideration than the children of royalty. These children are "the living images of Jesus Christ," and Lasallian educators should "honor Jesus Christ in their persons [Matthew 25:40]."

For De La Salle, all students were a proximate incarnation of Jesus Christ. "Recognize Jesus beneath the poor rags of the children whom you have to instruct. Adore him in them." Students may, at first, seem to be of limited ability and therefore perceived to be of limited value. But as human beings created by God their stature is much greater. The children that appear before the Lasallian educator are also described as "weary and exhausted travelers," "abandoned orphans" on the road of life seeking direction, support, and guidance in a confusing world. The sympathy that De La Salle has for them is evident in these reflections, a sense of compassion he urges others to adopt as well.

The Experience of Students

De La Salle was keenly aware of the situation in which children were being brought up among the poor and the working class of the cities of seventeenth-century France. More often than not they were largely neglected or ignored, allowed to amuse themselves in whatever way they wished until the lucky ones were able to begin working at some trade or craft while the rest joined the ranks of the working poor. Moral guidelines were loose or practically nonexistent. Each person was expected to survive on his or her own in an economy that was becoming increasingly powerful and individualistic. De La Salle realized that children were being educated by society into forms of thinking and behaving that would remain with them throughout their lives. That was why it was so important to shape their character in a Christian fashion at an early age.

Children, writes De La Salle:

seem to have no other inclination than to indulge their passions and their senses, and to satisfy their nature. . . . The way to free the soul of a child . . . then, is to make use of this remedy which will procure wisdom for him. If he is abandoned to his own will, he will run the risk of ruining himself and causing much sorrow to his parents. Faults committed will become habit and very difficult to correct. The good and bad habits contracted in childhood and maintained over a period of time ordinarily become second nature. . . . It can be said with real reason that a child who has acquired a habit of sin has more or less lost his freedom and has made himself miserable and captive.

Because of their sensitivity, "it is much easier for children to fall over some precipice, because they are weak in mind as well as body, and have little understanding of what is for their own good." It is not sufficient to merely teach children the knowledge they need and inculcate the dispositions they should have, they also "need the light of watchful guides to lead them . . . to help them to be aware of pitfalls and keep away from them."

De La Salle recognized that the parents of poor children rarely formed the religious dimension of their children's lives. They may have desired such formation and acknowledged its benefits, but they were often too occupied in making a living to engage in it themselves. As a result, the children who attended school "either have not had any instruction, or have been taught the wrong things, or, if they have received some good lessons, bad companions or their own bad habits have prevented them from benefiting." It was precisely with this vivid realization of their state that the Christian Schools worked toward procuring their salvation, a goal that included both immediate and long-range consequences.

The Approach Toward Student

In summary fashion, De La Salle points out the need to teach the young both spiritual and practical realities with a view toward cultivating "piety," a word that in the French means more than simply devotional practices.

> You will procure the good of the Church by making them true Christians and docile to the truths of faith and the maxims of the holy Gospel. You will procure the good of the state by teaching them how to read and write and everything else that pertains to your ministry in regard to exterior things. But piety should be joined to exterior things, otherwise your work would be of little use.

As much as possible, Lasallian educators strive to preserve the innocence of those entrusted to them, cultivating the virtue of purity, "a virtue so difficult to preserve in an age as corrupt as ours."

Lasallian educators are encouraged to "cultivate a very special tenderness" toward their disciples. "By the care you have for them show them how truly dear they are to you." The more affection is shown to them, especially toward the poor and less fortunate, the more they will be inspired through the teacher's efforts and "the more fully you will belong to Jesus Christ."

De La Salle had observed at numerous times that the "tendencies of the young are easily guided, so that they accept without great difficulty the impressions we seek to give them." This is why it is so important that the Lasallian educator "act so wisely in their regard that nothing in themselves or in their conduct could give these youths any dislike for the service of God, or cause them to deviate even slightly from their duties." Their approach

to students must be one of constant example, since this addresses their personal learning capacities and confirms the content of
one's teaching.

The most important approach that De La Salle advocates is
to "have recourse to God, knock on the door, pray, beg him insistently and even importunately" for the grace to live up to one's
vocation as a Lasallian educator.

> You have two sorts of children to instruct: some are dis-
> orderly and inclined to evil; the others are good, or at
> least inclined to good. Pray unceasingly for both . . .
> and especially for the conversion of those whose ten-
> dencies are evil. And work to preserve and strengthen
> the good ones in the practice of what is right. Still,
> make your care and your most fervent prayers strive to
> win over to God the hearts of those who are prone to
> evil.

The End Result in Students

Students give evidence to the Christian education they have received when "they often think of Jesus, their good and only Lord,
. . . often speak of Jesus,. . . long only for Jesus, and live only
for Jesus." They "practice what Jesus Christ has left us in the holy
Gospel." One finds in De La Salle's language an abiding desire to
make the person of Jesus Christ come alive to the students, so that
Jesus becomes for the students the same kind of operative presence that he has become for their teachers.

At the same time, the students "are beginning to be, and
one day should be perfect members" of the church. Such membership is shown in their docility to the truths of faith and the
maxims of the Gospel, along with piety and the spirit of religion.
Piety "is the principal object and the purpose of your work."
The full meaning of such "piety" revolves around the idea of
Christian maturity.

Students are also sent forth with a knowledge of all the practical truths and skills that will enable them to become responsible
members of society. Reading, writing, calculating, good manners,
pious example—all forms of knowledge that are useful to them—

have been given to them during the two or three years they have spent in the Christian School.

All of these fine results are brought to fulfillment in their holiness and in their union with Christ through the church. De La Salle is barely able to restrain his enthusiasm when he speaks about this, declaring that the Lasallian educator's concern is for

> making them holy, that all of them will arrive at the age of the perfect man and the fullness of Jesus Christ, so that they are no longer like children tossed here and there, carried about by every wind of doctrine, by deceit, and trickery . . . You are to help them in all things to grow up in Jesus Christ, who is their head, through whom the whole body of the Church holds its structure and its union, so that they may always be so united with the Church and in her that, by the hidden power of Jesus Christ furnished to all his members, [Ephesians 4:12–16] they will share in the promises of God in Jesus Christ [Ephesians 3:6].

THE TEACHER-STUDENT RELATIONSHIP

Based on a Moral Obligation

The relationship between the student and the teacher that De La Salle advocated is one that is based on a strong sense of moral obligation for the welfare of souls. There is no compromising or hedging on this issue. "It is God himself who. . . gives you responsibility to provide for all their spiritual needs. To do this should be your constant effort."

De La Salle minces no words in telling Lasallian educators how their personal spiritual growth and their conscientious practice of their ministry have ultimate consequences.

> Your duty requires you to teach [the students] religion. If they do not know it because you do not know it well yourself, or because you are careless in teaching it to them, you are false prophets. You are responsible for

making God known to them, yet you allow them to remain in an ignorance which may damn them, all because of your negligence.

By the responsibility that they have undertaken, Lasallian educators have given themselves to God in the place of those whom they instruct. "You have, so to speak, offered to him soul for soul." There can hardly be a more religiously intimate obligation than the one taken up under this conviction.

The starting point of the teacher-student relationship, then, is the conviction that the students' salvation is as important as, if not more important, than one's own. "On the day of judgment you will answer for them as much as you answer for yourselves....You must be convinced of this, that God will begin by making you give an account of their souls before asking you to give an account of your own."

With Properly Detached Perspective

The teacher-student relationship requires a gravity and a seriousness that reflects the nature of what is involved, and this must be communicated to the students by example. Lasallian educators provide an example to their students of self-control and reserve: "What they observe in you makes such an impression on them that it alone suffices to make them behave properly." In their earnest demeanor, such teachers provide all the preaching that should be necessary.

The properly detached perspective necessitated by the nature of the Lasallian educator's vocation is particularly applicable in the one area that De La Salle realized may be a key element in the entire educational enterprise—the correction of students. Correction is seen as impossible and ineffective unless teachers possess the authority, prudence, charity, and properly detached disposition of individuals whose aim is not punishment but correction.

There is no such thing as education without correction. Much of education, especially in the early years, consists largely of example and correction, whether this is in regard to skills or behavior. "It is typical of children that they often make mistakes by doing many things without thinking. Reproof and correction cause them to reflect on what they have to do and lead them to watch over themselves in order not to be making the same mistakes." If Lasallian educators are to correct their students effectively, they must have the kind of relationship with them that allows their corrections to be effective.

De La Salle uses the story of Nathan and David (2 Samuel 12: 1–9) to illustrate the nature of a prudent and wise form of correction. That example also "ought to make you realize how much good the corrections you give your disciples will accomplish, when they are given with gentleness and charity." The only effective form of correction is that which is given with complete detachment and thorough charity.

With Fraternally Attached Devotion

When De La Salle and the early teachers decided to call themselves "Brothers," they were describing their relationship to one another in community. But they also used this term explicitly to indicate the kind of relationship that would become the norm with students. Lasallian educators found themselves looked upon as older brothers of their students, benevolent ones to be sure. Their solicitude for the students' welfare and the care with which they attended to their duties resembled those of a serious older brother more than those of a schoolmaster. Perhaps De La Salle came to appreciate such a relationship when he found himself in charge of his three younger brothers after their parents had died. For several years, De La Salle himself supervised their education, striving to fulfill his responsibilities toward them in a way that was both serious and affectionate. This experience may have had some influence on his concern for the relationship between the Brothers and their students.

"You must . . . imitate God to some extent, for he . . . loved the souls he created." That imitation of God becomes incarnate in the teacher's daily relationship with students. "Every day you have poor children to instruct. Love them tenderly . . . following in this the example of Jesus Christ." Through such fraternal devotion and deep attachment to the good of their students, Lasallian educators are able to bring God's grace and love to those entrusted to their care. "Do you act in such a way as to have much kindness and affection for the children you teach? . . . The more tenderness you have for the members of Jesus Christ and of the Church who are entrusted to you, the more God will produce in them the wonderful effects of his grace."

Such tenderness is something beyond sentimentality or emotional attachment. It is a tenderness that leads them beyond the teacher-student relationship to a love of God, to "lead them to his holy love and to fill them with his Spirit." Such tenderness complements the more serious, firm side of the teaching relationship, evoking the more maternal aspects of the teaching vocation. "Do you take advantage of their affection for you to lead them to God? If you must have for them the firmness of a father to restrain and withdraw them from misbehavior, you must also have for them the tenderness of a mother to draw them to you and to do for them all the good that depends on you."

For Inspiring Genuine Piety

The relationship between teacher and student should inspire a true sense of piety in the students. By "piety" or Christian maturity, De La Salle means to indicate a broadly applied, deeply felt commitment to one's religious life. Even as Christianity pervaded seventeenth-century French society in ways almost unimaginable today, there still were many people who were largely unchurched, and it was common to find a great amount of immorality and licentiousness, especially in the cities. In advocating piety, De La Salle's primary concern is that students come to their full maturity as virtuous Christians in an often unvirtuous society. "Inspire them with love for virtue, impress upon them sentiments of piety, and see to it that God does not cease to reign in them."

Along with inspiring students to follow the Gospel maxims, the teachers are also held responsible for inspiring them to avoid anything that may lead them to sin. Practically minded as ever, De La Salle realized that inspiring goodness also required the honest perception of wickedness. Without the ability to recognize and avoid "occasions of sin," all the inspiration in the world would have no lasting effect. It is only when one is able to stay on the path to piety without straying off to the sides that the goal becomes realistically attainable.

For the teacher-student relationship to be one of inspiration, teachers must first be themselves inspired. Before a Lasallian educator is able to teach the Gospel maxims to students, "you must be thoroughly convinced of them yourself, so that you may impress them deeply on the hearts of your students. Make yourself docile, therefore, to the Holy Spirit, who can in a short time procure for you a perfect understanding of these truths."

All that the Lasallian educator does is oriented toward establishing the presence of the spirit of Jesus in the souls of the students. This is how true piety is expressed and established. "In a word, speak to them of everything that can lead them to piety. This is how your disciples should hear the voice of their teacher." Such piety "is the main benefit that you should impart to them, and the best gift you can give them when they leave you."

According to the Model of Jesus Christ and His Disciple

The idea of discipleship that defines the relationship between teacher and student is one that is informed by Jesus Christ's own example. De La Salle recommends the model of Jesus in the Gospels as the perfect example of the kind of teacher appropriate to a Christian School. By looking at the methods that Jesus used in leading his disciples to understand and practice the Gospel's truths, teachers will discover how they might similarly lead their own disciples toward the same goal. "In reading the Gospel you must study the manner and the means that Jesus used to lead his disciples to practice the truths of the Gospel."

Lasallian educators will find in Jesus' example all that they will need for winning the conversion of their students. It was part of the Brothers' *Rule* to carry a copy of the New Testament at all times and to read from it every day. Besides being the principal means by which the essential spirit of faith was to be cultivated, reading the Gospels from a teacher's perspective will show the way of teaching that Jesus manifested in his relationships with people. In the eyes of John Baptist de La Salle and his Brothers, that pedagogy is ultimately the ideal model for Christian instruction.

♥

4

De La Salle's Educational Practice

THE ACTIVITY OF TEACHING: THE VISION

Sharing in the Work of Salvation

The activity of teaching in the Christian School of De La Salle's time was one that "has for its purpose to procure the salvation of souls." It is an endeavor that imitates God's own, since God through zeal and affection sent Jesus Christ for just this purpose. God's own activity of salvation pervades the enterprise of teaching. It is the proximate means by which salvation reaches children. "Salvation" is to be found both in the efforts to make the students employable and in the growing maturity of their lives of faith.

As Jesus proclaimed the reign of God to his disciples through his teaching and example, so also is the Lasallian educator called "to establish and maintain the reign of God in the hearts of your students." Through means of example, religious instruction, genuine affection, and effective education, students are disposed toward responding to God's action in their lives and are led to receive God's reign in their hearts.

The teacher's vocation is to procure for children a "life of grace in this world and eternal life in the next." Such procurement is "doing God's work," following the model and example of Jesus' own ministry. "Keep, then, the goals of your work as completely pure as those of Jesus Christ." The teacher in the classroom, in effect, models Jesus Christ for the students. De La Salle urges teachers to "strive after the example of your divine master Jesus Christ to want only what God wants, when he wants it, and in the way he wants it."

In sharing in the work of salvation through one's teaching, one must also expect to share in the sufferings that such work inevitably brings about in this world. "Do not expect to receive any other reward than to suffer and to die as Jesus Christ did." De La Salle had no romantic notions about teaching the poor of France, especially the poor city youngsters whose experience must have included all sorts of cruel habits that they acquired as a means of survival. "The only thanks you should expect for instructing children, and especially the poor, is injury, insult, calumny, persecution, and even death." But one should patiently bear these sufferings without complaint, as the saints and Apostles did, since "the more faithful you are to God on occasions of suffering, the more God will pour out his graces and blessings on you in the exercise of your ministry."

But God does not leave teachers without consolation for their teaching endeavors. Those who have been assiduous in the exercise of their teaching can expect "an abundance of grace," "a larger field for their ministry, and a greater ability to procure the conversion of souls." Such rewards are different from those that might be expected, but they are commensurate with the nature of teaching as a salvific work. It is the same reward that Jesus and the Apostles found as a result of their endeavors.

Permeated by Faith

The activity of teaching is one that is imbued with the spirit of faith through and through. As a salvific work it is based on faith, done through faith, and engaged in for the sake of faith. God has given to teachers their vocation and "in consequence, desired and still desires that you find in it the way and the means of sanctifying yourself." The faith life of a Lasallian educator is realized essentially in the activity of teaching.

It is God's grace, God's loving gift of self, that enables the activity of authentic teaching. There is much that can be done simply through human effort and concern. But there is a great deal more that can be accomplished by working in cooperation with

God's grace. "Be satisfied with what you can do, since this satisfies God, but do not spare yourself in what you can do with the help of grace. Be convinced that, provided you are willing, you can do more with the help of God's grace than you imagine." Through the engagement of God's salvific presence, the Holy Spirit "who comes in a soul only to give it the life of grace and to cause it to act with grace," becomes an integral part of the teaching endeavor.

De La Salle was ever aware of the difficulties that were encountered in the classroom and the challenges presented to his teachers on a daily basis. The invoking of God's grace through interior prayer was no mere panacea for enduring those difficulties but rather an essential, effective means of transforming such difficulties into opportunities for mediating God's salvation. "Be assured that the more you devote yourself to prayer, the more you will also do well in your work. For you are not of yourself able to do anything effective for the salvation of souls. Therefore, you should often turn to God to obtain from [God] what your profession obliges you to give to others."

The activity of teaching in the Christian School "will succeed only in so far as we are aided by God's help and directed by the Holy Spirit." Lasallian educators must ask God earnestly that all instruction "be given life by the Spirit and draw all their power from God." Only by such means will teaching resonate with God's own life so that "those who belong to God may have life and have it more abundantly."

Joining Zeal with Action

"When we are called to an apostolic mission, if we do not join zeal to action all we do for our neighbor will have little effect." The activity of teaching requires great zeal, both in the face of opposition and in the daily requirements of the classroom. "Let your zeal give tangible proof that you love those whom God has entrusted to you just as Jesus Christ has loved his Church."

An active zeal does not manifest itself in frenetic activity or constant correction. It is found in a continual awareness and involvement in the activity of teaching; one's attention doesn't wander or become distracted by personal concerns—surely a challenging task.

One of the most direct ways that zeal in action is manifest is through the vigilance that the Lasallian educator exercises over students. Instruction is not sufficient; one must also watch over the students' conduct. Vigilance comprises both an ever ready willingness to step in and correct an offending situation, and an ability to lead students to practice the good they are capable of practicing.

De La Salle noted "interior and exterior enemies" that work in opposition to the growth of piety. Vigilance includes a zealous effort to prevent the victory of such "enemies." Two examples of these are bad companions and bad habits. "One of the main things that most contributes to the corruption of young people is keeping bad company. Few go astray from malice of heart. The majority are perverted by bad example and by the circumstances that they encounter." See to it "that they associate only with good ones. Thus being exposed to none but good impressions they will practice what is right with great ease." De La Salle here captures the influence that peer pressure can have and turns its dynamics into a force in support of the activity of teaching.

Similarly, the bad habits that students pick up during their youth are often quite difficult to break. It is "by your gentleness and wisdom that you lead those entrusted in your care to give up bad habits and disorderly conduct." One can only inspire the acquisition of good habits by modeling them. It would be useless to angrily denounce bad habits, since this displays the same fault that one is trying to correct. Instead, "when attempts are made to entice your pupils to do evil, strengthen them in doing good." It is not enough to prevent students from wrong behavior in the teacher's presence, one must also "show them how to avoid all other occasions of evil when they are no longer under your supervision."

Marked by Individual Care

Even though De La Salle is credited with the effective use of the simultaneous method on the primary level, this does not mean that he was not concerned about students' individual capacities. The activity of teaching that he recommends to his followers constantly bears the various abilities of students in mind. If they are not taught properly, the fault lies not with them but with the teachers. Each student is seen as an individual with both capacities appropriate to the student's age and requirements particular to the student's personality. Teaching that did not recognize this would be unsuccessful, whether it were according to the simultaneous method or according to any other method. De La Salle writes,

> One of the main concerns of those who instruct others is to be able to understand their students and to discern the right way to guide them. They must show more mildness toward some, more firmness toward others. There are those who call for much patience, those who need to be stimulated and spurred on, some who need to be reproved and punished to correct them of their faults, others who must be constantly watched over to prevent them from being lost or going astray. This guidance requires understanding and discernment of spirits, qualities you should frequently and earnestly ask of God, for they are most necessary for you in the guidance of those placed in your care.

Teachers must help their students practice all "the good that is appropriate to their years." Students are expected to learn "according to their age and ability" and not according to some predetermined standard imposed on everyone.

Lasallian educators were not to "show favoritism toward others because they were rich, or pleasant, or naturally possessing more lovable qualities than the others." In fact, those who were poor, more disposed to evil inclinations, and who possessed unfavorable qualities were to be attended to with greater care since they were the ones in greatest need. But undue familiarity with students was to be avoided as well. The activity of teaching should include an element of disinterestedness that shows no partiality to anyone but rather admires in students those qualities of piety and virtue that are expected from them and are being taught to them.

Engaged in Touching Hearts

De La Salle's favorite image for the activity of teaching is the winning and the touching of hearts. "You carry out a work that requires you to touch hearts." Such an image captures the essentially interior nature of teaching. Facts and figures have neither the formative power nor comprise the major component of

A 19th century painting by Jean-Joseph Lacroix, "Brothers' Pupils Leaving Church After Mass," that illustrates some of the guidelines found in *The Conduct of Schools*.

the activity of teaching. True teaching involves dynamics of the heart, as salvation itself does. The salvation of souls is a matter of touching hearts, of leading children to live in a Christian manner through winning their hearts. Failing to do this will not only fail to draw them to God but will instead drive them away. Therefore, Lasallian educators have the duty "of learning how to touch hearts" and often ask for the grace to do so.

Children "themselves are a letter which Christ dictates to you, which you write each day in their hearts, not with ink, but by the Spirit of the living God." Children have an openness, a capacity for learning and for inspiration. They are like a letter waiting to be written, ready for the kind of personal communication from God that the Lasallian educator provides. These teachers may be the first encounter that children have of God's loving concern for them. Along with learning how to write, students come to know the foundation out of which writing receives its power. By touching their hearts, writing Christ's Gospel with the Spirit of the living God, Lasallian educators awaken and enkindle in the hearts of students their ability to participate in their heritage as children of God.

Such work requires faith. "Do you have such faith that it is able to touch the hearts of your students and to inspire them with the Christian spirit? This is the greatest miracle you could perform, and the one that God asks of you, since this is the purpose of your work."

One of the means whereby hearts are touched is the example of virtue. De La Salle himself touched the hearts of teachers, students, fellow clerics, and many with whom he came into contact. His life of virtue impressed a host of individuals, and he obtained a reputation for being able to convert the most hardened of sinners. De La Salle captures the principle in a nutshell when he writes: "Virtue cannot hide. When it is seen it is attractive, and the example it gives makes such a strong impression on those who witness it practiced or who hear it spoken about, that most people are led to imitate it." It is the full measure of one's conduct and behavior that touches the hearts of one's disciples. The activity of teaching finds its life in this touching of hearts.

THE ACTIVITY OF TEACHING: THE PRACTICE

The large groups of pupils that occupied the Christian Schools from the schools' inception necessitated a method of instruction radically different from the commonly used individualized tutorial method. Coping with classes of up to a hundred small boys would be sheer chaos without a system of organization that addressed their common educational needs even as it considered each of their individual academic situations. A large supply of trained teachers was not available for smaller classes. De La Salle's detailed pedagogical plan made maximum use of a trained teacher among the largest number of students in order to provide the specific educational requirements of generally available elementary education.

The major teaching components that illustrate De La Salle's more universal educational convictions include his use of the simultaneous method, his practical perspective exemplified in the use of the vernacular, and his inclusion of various elements of individualized attention.

The Simultaneous Method

The general principle of simultaneous instruction is described in the *Conduct* as follows: "All students of the same grade will . . . follow the lessons together, without distinction or discrimination, as the teacher will require of them. . . . All the students of each grade will have the same book and have the same lesson together." Each classroom consisted of a number of levels and grades together, each group of students following its own program of activities. Each group would be addressed in turn by the teacher, with the other groups quietly working on their own material.

In reading, for example, one student reads while all are reading the same material to themselves, the teacher calling on students out of turn in order to make sure that they are following the same section. In arithmetic, individual pupils do examples of particular lessons for the class, being questioned by the teacher to make sure that each concept and term is fully understood. Everything explained to the pupil should be repeated by the pupil before moving on. If the one doing the example fails in any respect, another student doing the same lesson is called on to make the correction, or failing that, a student doing a more advanced lesson is called on. After each correction, the original student repeats the correct answer. Every single student is to do an example on the board of the lesson being covered, with the teacher paying close attention to both what the student does and says.

In the teaching of religion, the entire class was addressed by the teacher, who asked a series of questions and subquestions. Care was taken that no answers were suggested to students either partially or wholly by other students. Students helped others best by providing correct answers when called on.

Integral to De La Salle's method was the policy of personally involving each student every day. Every student experienced direct contact with the teachers. Some students were called on a number of times, especially those whose attention tended to wander or those who needed greater reinforcement. The *Conduct* makes no provision for volunteering answers; no raising of hands, for example. Simultaneous instruction clearly proceeded from the teacher. Everyone took part in the educational process directly, but they did so under the complete direction of the teacher, who determined at the end of each month which students should be promoted.

This engraving by F. Vouvin from 1873 is a somewhat severe illustration of the class arrangements laid out by the *Conduct of Schools* from a late 19th century perspective.

Practical Perspectives and Using the Vernacular

John Baptist de La Salle was a thoroughly practical individual. Even while his religious vision inspired the work of the schools, practical concerns brought that vision into reality. Some examples of De La Salle's practical sense are that schools were designed with good ventilation and light sources, and windows were located high enough so that no one from the outside could look in (and *vice versa)*. De La Salle's text on Christian politeness was published in an elaborate script form, so that when students were ready to read it, they would not only learn societal conventions of behavior but would be further challenged by a formal writing style that they would encounter as adults. Advanced spelling and writing students would learn to spell and copy common written forms used in society such as bills, contracts, business letters, and other practical documents. Arithmetic concentrated on the French monetary system. On the way to the local parish Mass, teachers walked on the opposite side of the street from the marching rows of students, noting their behavior and never correcting them until before leaving for Mass on the following day. A young teacher was supervised by an older one who was either in the same classroom or teaching next door with the door open between the two classrooms. For each school activity, De La Salle and the teachers considered the most practical means of accomplishing their goal, and then set out to do it. The use of French in teaching was a particularly far-reaching case in point.

Learning to read French by learning to read Latin had long been the French practice, dating from the Middle Ages when future clerics were virtually the only ones educated at monastery and cathedral schools. Later on, it was presumed that since Latin was phonetically spelled, it was initially more easily read. Children would not be taught to understand the Latin sentences, only how to read them out loud correctly. Based on this knowledge, they would learn how to read in French.

But De La Salle reasoned that given the short time poor students had to learn anything at all, and the vast advantage French had over Latin in everyday life, the schools should teach the reading of French directly. Since French was the students' mother tongue, they could already speak and understand it. Learning Latin at this stage would cause nothing but educational, social, and personal difficulties that are just as easily avoided by the direct learning of French.

De La Salle's schools taught reading through nine stages, beginning with the alphabet and French syllables, then moving through graded French texts, ending with De La Salle's book on Christian politeness. Prior to this last French text, students also learned how to pronounce the Latin texts of the psalter, primarily for the sake of participating in church. The teaching of the vernacular, however, was first in order and in importance. It was this practice, along with the effective use of the simultaneous method, that differentiated the Christian Schools most notably from other educational enterprises of the time.

Elements of Individualized Attention

The simultaneous method of instruction may seem mechanized, impersonal, and constricting to the eyes of some educational theorists, but within the appropriate setting and with trained teachers it became a method that was much more successful, and finally much more individually oriented, than the prevailing individualized tutorial method. Certain practices highlight this concern for individuals.

Each teacher drew up a record for each student in class. This record began with a family interview when the pupil was admitted, recording his family, background, home life, particular traits, and other significant data. During the year, the teacher would enter pertinent information about the student, passing it to the next teacher at the end of the year. When the student left, the information would be filed for future reference. A sample of one such file reads as follows:

> Francis Delevieux: 8 1/2, two years at school, in 3rd section of Writing since July 1st. Somewhat turbulent; little piety at church or prayers unless supervised. Lacks reserve. Conduct satisfactory; needs encouragement to effort; punishment of no avail; light-headed. Rarely absent except when with bad companions; often late. Ap-

plication moderate but he learns with ease. Twice near-
ly send down for negligence. Submissive to a strong
hand. Not a difficult character. Must be won over.
Spoilt at home. Parents resent his being punished.

Notably, such records understood that teaching was a profession that required the careful observation of individual characteristics and particular sensibilities. As with physicians, lawyers,
bankers, and other professionals, careful record keeping insured
that services were geared to individual people in specific situations.
Students were also involved in school and classroom management. If there was a job to be done in school, there was a student
to do it. Such duties with their qualifications and terms of office
were carefully described, rotated among the pupils either as a reward or as an incentive toward developing responsibility. Leaders
of prayers did so throughout the day. Holy water bearers made
holy water available when entering or leaving church. The rosary
keeper and his assistants gave rosaries out in class and in church,
distributing them and counting them when returned. The bell
ringer had to be vigilant, exact, and punctual, ringing the bell each
half hour and at the beginning and end of the school day. Papers
were given out and returned by students who followed a set routine. The doorkeeper saw to it that only teachers, pupils, and the
parish priest were admitted. The keeper of the key opened the
school for pupils thirty minutes prior to the arrival of the teachers,
making sure that everything in the school was as it had been left.
A class inspector observed all that went on while teachers were absent from their classrooms (primarily before school), reporting
everything to the teacher and never interfering with whatever was
happening in any way. Two "undercover" monitors of the inspector insured that this office was carried out without compromise.
There were also supervisors for the main streets where students
lived, making sure students weren't behaving inappropriately when
coming from or going to school and generally keeping the teachers aware of the students' behavior. Such duties as these helped individual pupils develop a good sense of responsibility and generally
facilitated the fair treatment of all the children in accordance with
their age and personal characteristics.

The teachers were also aware of individual limitations and sensitivities in the classroom. Students who had difficulty in remembering and who were less intelligent were called on more frequently. Pupils were not permitted to laugh at the answer of another or prompt someone who was unable to answer. When a student could not give a full answer, the question was to be divided into parts so that the answer could be given in smaller sections.

In the manner of asking students questions, one of the major ways in which education took place, individual abilities were accounted for as well.

> In the questions, the teacher will make use of only the simplest expressions and words which are very easily understood and need no explanation, if this is possible making the questions as short as possible. . . . Teachers will plan that the questions, the subquestions, and the answers to the subquestions fulfill the following four conditions: (1) they must be short; (2) they must make complete sense; (3) they must be accurate; and (4) the answers must be suited to the capacity of the average and not of the most able and most intelligent students, so that the majority may be able to answer the questions that are asked of them.

THE SCHOOL: THE VISION

All De La Salle's efforts were directed toward the good running of Christian Schools. De La Salle included little in his meditations on the schools *per se*, since the particular aspects of the running of schools were fully outlined in the *Conduct*. He did, however, offer some significant general insights on the school in both the *Meditations* and the *Conduct*.

Why Have Christian Schools?

In his *Meditations for the Time of Retreat* De La Salle drew the "big picture" of the Christian Schools for his teachers. He had already stated elsewhere that the Lasallian educators' work, insofar as they were participating in the work of Christ and the Apostles, "is the same as that of the institute founded by Saint Ignatius, which is the salvation of souls." The way whereby this was accomplished—the gratuitous education of the poor in Christian Schools—bore its own mark.

> God is so good that, having created man, he wills that all come to the knowledge of truth [1 Timothy 2:4]. This truth is God himself and what he has desired to reveal to us through Jesus Christ, through his holy apostles, and through his Church. This is why God wills all to be instructed, so that their minds may be enlightened by the light of faith.
>
> We cannot be instructed in the mysteries of our religion unless we have the good fortune to hear about them, and we cannot have this advantage unless someone preaches the word of God.
>
> . . . Consider that it is only too common for the working class and the poor to allow their children to live on their own, roaming all over like vagabonds until they are able to be put to some work. These parents have no concern to send their children to school because they are too poor to pay teachers, or else they have to go out to look for work and perforce abandon their children.
>
> The results of this condition are regrettable, for these poor children, accustomed to lead an idle life for many years, have great difficulty adjusting when it comes time for them to go to work. In addition, through association with bad companions they learn to commit many sins which later on are very difficult to stop, the bad habits having been contracted over so long a period of time.
>
> God has had the goodness to remedy so great a misfortune by the establishment of the Christian Schools, where the teaching is offered free of charge and entirely for the glory of God, where children are kept during

the day and learn reading, writing, and their religion. In these schools the children are always kept busy, so that when their parents want them to go to work, they are prepared for employment.

The Christian Schools have been established in answer to God's call and in the face of the great need for such institutions within society. They arise out of God's provident care for humanity. Such schools answer the needs of students as they answer the needs of their parents, providing practical training and religious formation. By means of Christian Schools, God's plan of salvation is able to be realized in this particular society for these particular members of that society.

Community Aspects of the Schools

It made a difference that Christian Schools in the seventeenth-century were run by a religious community of laymen dedicated to gratuitous education for the glory of God and the salvation of souls. This was a common work done by a single group under a united vision. In order to be effective in that work, so as to exemplify and inspire the general atmosphere of the schools, the teachers were urged to work in "union of mind and heart."

Although De La Salle never referred to the school as a "community," the posture that the Brothers as a community held vis-à-vis the school made a real difference, a difference that would have its parallel in a current school faculty's sense of community. Some of what De La Salle had to say about how Brothers should treat one another applies equally to a school faculty. For example, individuals should carry one another's burdens, whether those hardships be personality traits or particular idiosyncratic behaviors. Such charity is very advantageous in a community, since "a community where charity and union are lacking is a kind of hell." The rule that De La Salle suggested for community living fits as appropriately in the community of the school: "Never speak except in a kindly manner. When you fear to fail in this, remain silent."

Lasallian education in De La Salle's time was also entirely gratuitous. The Brothers were absolutely forbidden to receive any gifts, favors, or keepsakes from the students or their parents—especially tobacco. This not only guaranteed an equal relationship with all students, it also maintained De La Salle's conviction that gratuitous instruction was the sole means of effectively and convincingly accomplishing the ends of Christian education.

School Characteristics

Three characteristics of the school that were reflected in the meditations should be highlighted. First, schools were places where the young did not have to associate with bad companions. It was there that they might "become close friends with the best of their companions, the most pious, and the best behaved." Such beneficial associations would hopefully be carried on outside of the school and would contribute to the development of Christian virtue.

Second, schools were places where teaching was conscientiously, effectively, and affectionately carried out. One of the meditations proceeds through a long list of questions that inquires into whether or not the teachers followed the lessons closely, corrected their pupils promptly, taught catechism and religion every day, wasted time or acted in a careless way, chatted to the children uselessly, and accepted anything from them. One clearly gets the impression that not a stone was to be left unturned in the establishment of well-run Christian Schools.

Third, schools were places where proper correction became a normal, charitable dimension of educational activity. In families as in society, behavior might be corrected through various means, was often cruel (for example, branding the arm of a youngster who stole with the letter "V" for *"volure / thief"* was a common practice) or was more often entirely neglected. But in the schools, the teachers were ever vigilant over their students, ready to correct them with both proper measures and personal example. The welfare of the student was of foremost concern. No correction was administered unless its benefit was clearly evident to both teacher and student. "Men, and even children, are endowed with reason and

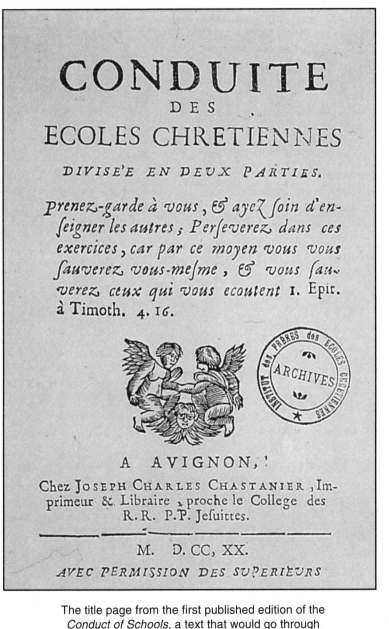

CONDUITE

DES

ECOLES CHRETIENNES

DIVISE'E EN DEUX PARTIES.

prenez-garde à vous, & ayez soin d'enseigner les autres ; Perseverez dans ces exercices, car par ce moyen vous vous sauverez vous-mesme, & vous sauverez ceux qui vous ecoutent I. Epit. à Timoth. 4. 16.

A AVIGNON,

Chez JOSEPH CHARLES CHASTANIER, Imprimeur & Libraire, proche le College des R. R. P.P. Jesuittes.

M. D. CC, XX.

AVEC PERMISSION DES SUPERIEURS

The title page from the first published edition of the
Conduct of Schools, a text that would go through
over 20 editions during the next 200 years.

must not be corrected like animals, but like reasonable persons. . . . We must reprove and correct with justice, and so we must help children to recognize the wrong they have done, to understand the correction which their fault deserves, and we must try to have them agree to it."

De La Salle also cited the religious parameters that encompassed this most necessary school dimension. "Take care, above all, that it is charity and zeal for the salvation of the souls of your pupils that lead you to correct them." Otherwise, one might lead them away from God. The proper, appropriate exercise of correction was one of the most effective ways of guiding the spiritual growth of the young. De La Salle saw it as one of the most central characteristics of the Christian Schools.

THE SCHOOL: THE PRACTICES

The Role of Discipline

The guidelines from De La Salle's meditations listed above are only general principles to consider in the administration of school discipline. The entire second part of the *Conduct* gives the details by specifying the means needed to maintain good order in school, with a long section on the administration of discipline that contains multiple detailed criteria. A simple listing of the topics covered in the *Conduct* gives a good idea of the major concerns.

MEANS OF ESTABLISHING AND MAINTAINING ORDER IN THE SCHOOLS

CHAPTER I: THE VIGILANCE WHICH THE TEACHER MUST SHOW IN SCHOOL

- Care Which a Teacher Should Take in Correcting Words and the Proper Manner of Doing So
- Care Which the Teacher Should Take to Make All the Students Having the Same Lesson Follow It
- Care Which the Teacher Must Take to Enforce Silence in School

CHAPTER II: SIGNS WHICH ARE USED IN THE CHRISTIAN SCHOOLS

- Signs Used During Meals
- Signs Concerning Lessons
- Signs Used in the Writing Lesson
- Signs Used During Catechism and Prayers
- Signs Used in Reference to Corrections
- Signs That Are Used Only on Special Occasions

CHAPTER III: RECORDS OR REGISTERS

- Record of Promotions in Lessons
- Record Levels in Lessons

CHAPTER IV: REWARDS

CHAPTER V: INTRODUCTORY REMARKS ON CORRECTION IN GENERAL

- Different Kinds of Corrections
- Correction by Words
- Correction with the Ferule
- Correction with the Rod
- Expulsion of Students from School
- Frequent Correcting and How to Avoid Them
- Qualities Which Corrections Should Possess
- Faults Which Must Be Avoided in Corrections
- Children Who Must or Must Not Be Corrected
- Ill-bred and Self-willed or Delinquent Children
- Stubborn Students
- Children Who Have Been Gently Reared and Those of a Timid Disposition
- Accusers and Accused
- What the Practice Should Be in All These Methods of Correcting Penances: Their Use, Their Qualities, and the Manner of Imposing Them
- List of Penances Which Are in Use and Can Be Imposed on the Students for Certain Faults

CHAPTER VI: ABSENCES

- Regular Absences and Absences With Permission
- Irregular Absences and Those that May or May Not be Permitted
- The Causes of Absences and the Means of Preventing Them
- How and by Whom Absentees Should be Received and Their Absences Excused

CHAPTER VII: HOLIDAYS

- Ordinary Holidays
- Extraordinary Holidays
- Vacation
- Manner of Informing Teachers and Students of Holidays

CHAPTER VIII: SCHOOL OFFICERS

- The Reciter of Prayer; The Holy Water Bearer; The Rosary Carrier and Assistants; The Bell Ringer; The Monitors and Supervisors; The Observers; The Distributors and Collectors of Papers; The Sweepers; The Doorkeeper; The Keeper of the School Key

CHAPTER IX: CONSTRUCTION AND UNIFORMITY OF SCHOOLS

- The Furniture Which They Contain

The Twelve Virtues of a Good Teacher

When considering the issue of discipline in Christian Schools of seventeenth-century France, one needs to keep in mind that the use of harsh corporal punishment on the elementary level was routine and frequent. Michel de Montaigne, the French essayist, describes one educational establishment as "a real house of correction for imprisoned youth . . . [Y]ou shall hear nothing but the outcries of the boys under execution, with the thundering noise of their pedagogues drunk with fury." (In Battersby, 1949, p. 95)

Such a situation was commonly accepted at the time. King Louis XIV himself had been subject to the use of corporal punishment and saw it as part of educational life, as did most of France.

De La Salle, however, realized that piety and religion were not fostered by punishment. The need for punishment should be reduced as much as possible by a variety of factors that should make its use rare. Teachers were to "be careful to punish their pupils but rarely, being persuaded that this is one of the principal ways of regulating a school properly and of establishing very good order." The overall atmosphere of the school that was created by its organized methodology, the seriousness of its teachers, the religious character of all its operations, the deliberate and respectful silence within its buildings; all contributed to a situation where the use of punishment was a clear exception to common practice.

De La Salle realized, however, that on the practical level punishment was a reality in elementary education. A class full of young boys, no matter how silent or how well-organized, would need correcting now and then. Experience had shown him that teachers must act in a manner both gentle and firm, showing the gravity of a father and never letting passion or anger have part in the correction. In all cases, "No correction that could be harmful to the one who is to receive it must ever be administered. This would be to act directly contrary to the purpose of correction, which has been instituted only to do good."

Nothing was left to chance in the administration of school discipline. The *Conduct* is filled with sound advice in this respect. In fact, some of the advice that he gives is extremely unusual for the historical time period, revealing an educational wisdom that deeply respects the integrity of both teachers and students. Six ways are given in which the *teacher* can be unbearable to the students. They are presented here in full to highlight the remarkable insight behind them.

- First, the teacher's penances are too rigorous and the yoke which the teacher imposes upon the students is too heavy. This state of affairs is frequently due to lack of discretion and judgment on the part of the teacher. It often happens that students do not have enough strength of body or of mind to bear the burdens which many times overwhelm them.

- Second, when the teacher enjoins, commands, or exacts something of the children with words too harsh and in a manner too domineering. Above all, the teacher's conduct is unbearable when it arises from unrestrained impatience or anger.
- Third, when the teacher is too insistent in urging upon a child some performance which the child is not disposed to do, and the teacher does not permit the child the leisure or the time to reflect.
- Fourth, when the teacher exacts little things and big things alike with the same ardor.
- Fifth, when the teacher immediately rejects the reasons and excuses of children and is not willing to listen to them at all.
- Sixth, when the teacher is not mindful enough of personal faults that he does not know how to sympathize with the weaknesses of children and so exaggerates their faults too much. This is the situation when the teacher reprimands them or punishes them and acts as though dealing with an insensible instrument rather than with a creature capable of reason.

Similarly, there were six ways in which the teacher's weakness leads to laxity:

- First, care is taken by the teacher only about things that are important and which cause disorder, and when other less important matters are imperceptibly neglected.
- Second, when not enough insistence is placed upon the performance and observance of the school practices and those things which constitute the duties of the children.
- Third, when children are easily permitted to neglect what has been prescribed.
- Fourth, when, in order to preserve the friendship of the children, a teacher shows too much affection and

tenderness to them. This involves granting something special or giving too much liberty to the more intimate. This does not edify the others, and it causes disorder.

- Fifth, when, on account of the teacher's natural timidity, the children are addressed or reprimanded so weakly or so coldly that they do not pay any attention or that the correction makes no impression upon them.

- Sixth and final, a teacher easily forgets proper deportment, which consists principally in maintaining a gravity which encourages respect and restraint on the part of the children. This lack of deportment manifests itself either in speaking to the students too often and too familiarly or in doing some undignified act.

There is also a detailed section on the kinds of children who should and who should not be punished. Discrimination in this case is essential, since everyone is not alike. Here, De La Salle shows a keen eye for the emotional dynamics to which children are subject, and he wants to make sure that corrections indeed accomplish what they should; that is, to correct wrong behavior. The *Conduct* speaks of children who get little attention at home, those who are bold, insolent, frivolous, stubborn in various ways, timid, gently reared, simple-minded, little, or sickly. In some cases, such as the stubborn, correction should always be used, but in many of these cases it should be applied judiciously or not at all. All these detailed prescriptions are meant to insure that "firmness may not degenerate into harshness and that gentleness may not degenerate into languor and weakness."

These disciplinary measures would not have been maintained had they not been successful. As poor or frequent use of discipline leads to a dislike of teachers and the school, so also a moderate and fair use of it produces the opposite effect. The general favorable opinion of the schools by the public at large attested to the degree of success that the schools that utilized these specific measures and general principles enjoyed.

The Influence of Silence

Silence was a cardinal factor in the management of the Christian Schools. Visitors to the schools could hardly believe the silence that pervaded an institution where up to five hundred small boys were being taught. De La Salle's early biographer, Canon Blain, a contemporary of De La Salle's, wrote,

> [The visitors'] surprise increased when, on entering, they beheld the teacher amid this multitude of light-headed pupils, all as quiet as if they were an audience listening to the sermon of an eloquent preacher. Struck by such a novel spectacle, they have stayed for hours, motionless and attentive, hearing the children read, watching the signs of the teacher correcting their mistakes, and admiring the order and silence which reigned there.

The students' voices carried the education. By making silence the rule, rather than the exception, the focus was placed on learning rather than on verbose teaching.

"Silence is one of the principal means of establishing and maintaining order in schools." Teachers are to speak rarely with students in class, and "when they speak, teachers will do so very seriously and in few words." This, however, did not mean that there was little communication in the classroom. The activity of teaching was defined by interaction, hence there should be some means whereby such interaction can occur. But the kind of interaction appropriate to elementary education in the seventeenth-century bears little outward resemblance to that appropriate to elementary education today. In De La Salle's time, such interaction was largely regimented and nonverbal.

> As there are many occasions on which teachers are obliged to speak, a great many signs have been established in the Christian Schools. To make it easier for teachers to keep silence and to reduce these signs to some order, the signs have been classified according to those practices and activities which most ordinarily oc-

cur in schools. A pointer-like instrument used by the Brothers and called the "signal" is employed to give most of these signs.

Some signs were obvious, such as tapping on a text to indicate that students should prepare to read. Others were more obscure, such as moving a raised hand from the right to the left to indicate to the students that they should assume a better posture in their seats. The pointer-like signal was used most often, the teacher indicating specific behaviors by clicking it, pointing it, and waving it about in all sorts of ways. In many cases, the signs involved direct eye contact followed by a modeling gesture on the part of the teacher or a series of clicks that had specified meanings in a set pattern depending on the subject being studied. One full chapter of the Conduct is dedicated to an exposition of these signs and signals.

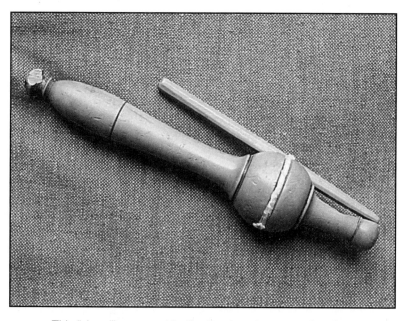

This "signal" was used by the teachers to ensure that they spoke very little during class and that student voices were the primary ones that were heard.

Silence had been recommended by Charles Démia for the schools of Lyons, but De La Salle almost raised it to an art form in the Christian Schools. The reasons for this silent context for teaching weren't only practical. Schools reflected a characteristic that De La Salle had cultivated in himself all his life, the silent presence of God in the world and in one's self. If nothing else, to the world outside the classrooms, it was the quiet atmosphere pervading the Christian Schools that identified them most immediately.

A Reserved Attitude of Respect

The last component of the activity of teaching that stood out in Christian Schools was the reserve and respect displayed by teachers and students in class. Teachers never touched students, and explicitly not while giving correction. Their presence always communicated seriousness and fraternal concern. All their efforts were focused on performing their tasks in a manner worthy of their demanding vocation.

> Teachers . . . will be careful to maintain a very modest demeanor and to act with great seriousness. They will never allow themselves to descend to anything unbecoming or to act in a childish fashion, such as to laugh or to do anything that might excite the students. The seriousness demanded of teachers does not consist in having a severe or austere aspect, in getting angry, or in saying harsh words. It consists of great reserve in their gestures, in their actions, and in their words. Teachers will above all be cautious not to become too familiar with the students, not to speak to them in an easy manner, and not to allow the students to speak to them other than with great respect.

Such serious demeanor did not mean the lack of all personal concern between teacher and student. Sufficient references to De La Salle's meditations and the concerns for students shown in the *Conduct* have already firmly established the health and depth of the teacher's relationship with the students. Canon Blain wrote,

Among the blessings bestowed by God on the work of the Brothers, we must count the affection which the pupils show toward them. Often, even in those places where the Brothers have suffered persecution, as in Paris and Rouen, small children have been seen running out of their homes, from their mothers' arms or from their childish games, to greet the Brothers with outstretched arms as if wishing to embrace them, and crying out, "Here are the Brothers, here are the Brothers."

In fact it may be that the reserve with which these teachers engaged in their work contributed to the regard the students had for them, insofar as the students knew and experienced a kind of respect, attention, fair treatment, and interest in their welfare that they hardly experienced anywhere else. At the same time, De La Salle knew that one's outside demeanor made a difference, as when he admonishes one Brother in a letter: "Your Brothers complain that they never see you in a good mood, and they all say that you look like a prison door."

The Place of Religion in the School

One could not speak about the pedagogy of John Baptist de La Salle without identifying the place of religion in the school. It may seem obvious from what has been said already that religion is the Christian School's primary concern. But there are two points that must be emphasized: (1) Christian instruction, as the school's first work, comes about by both indirect and direct means, and (2) a Christian School is consequently not a catechetical center nor are its teachers primarily or solely catechists.

Christian Instruction: Both Direct and Indirect

Christian Schools were not given their name only to distinguish them from the poorly-run parish charity schools and the non-gratuitous Little Schools. "Christian" in France at the time meant "Roman Catholic." Calling a school a "Christian" School stressed the religious dimension of education, the religious preoccupation of its curriculum, and the fundamental religious purpose of its establishment. The 1705 *Rule* stated,

The end of this Institute is to give a Christian education to children; it is for this purpose the Brothers keep
schools, that having children under their care from
morning until evening, they may teach them to lead
good lives, by instructing them in the mysteries of our
holy religion and by inspiring them with Christian
maxims, and thus give them a suitable education.

All that the teachers did, they did to form committed Cath-
olics who were genuine disciples of Jesus Christ. Schools were
structured to provide an atmosphere where this could take place,
and teachers were trained to bring this about with the greatest
care and assiduity. The major reasons for De La Salle's success
arose out of the implicit and explicit religious curriculum that the
Christian Schools implemented.

Explicitly, the daily half-hour of religious instruction, which
included a short "reflection" by the teacher on some point of faith
or morality, was considered the most important instruction of the
day. The subject matter came from the catechism of the Diocese,
and the Brothers prepared their religion lessons using the volumes
of *The Duties of a Christian* that De La Salle wrote. The manner in
which the teachers were to teach these religious duties reveals how
well De La Salle knew the learning capacities of young children.

Teachers will speak only on the subject assigned for the
day and will guard against departing from it. . . .
They will never say anything vulgar or anything that
might cause laughter, and will be careful not to speak
in a dull way which could produce weariness. In every
lesson teachers will be sure to indicate some practices to
the students. . . . Care must be taken not to disturb
the Catechism lesson by untimely reprimands and corrections. . . . On Sundays and holy days, when the
Catechism lasts three times as long as on the other
days, teachers will always choose some story that the
students will enjoy, and will tell it in a way that will
please them and renew their attention with details that
will prevent the students from being bored.

Besides the religion lesson, each day included multiple prayers, attendance at the local parish Mass, and applications of Gospel maxims by the teacher as occasions warranted, reinforcing specific Gospel principles or teachings.

Implicitly, classroom pictures that were fully described in the *Conduct* and the texts used for the lessons reinforced the Christian atmosphere of the school. Of course, the teacher conducted himself with a reserve that, in his person, spoke of the school's religious ends. The teaching methodology was thoroughly infused with the religious dynamism of the Gospels.

De La Salle realized that "no matter how much faith they may have, nor how lively it may be, if [the students] are not practicing any good works at all, their faith will be of no use to them." Everything possible, then, was done to lead students to practice the virtues they were taught. The practical truths of the Gospel were taught not only by words but also by example, not only by command but also by invitation, not by any one activity but by a multitude of "teachable moments" throughout the school day.

MORE THAN CATECHETICAL CENTERS AND CATECHISTS

It should be clear by now that the kinds of goals that the Christian Schools set out to accomplish could not have been achieved without an integrated approach that educated the whole person. Christian instruction came about through much more than the religion lesson or through the explicitly religious activities of the day. It was the *Christian School* that accomplished this instruction through trained, dedicated Christian teachers.

Proportionally, more time was spent teaching reading, writing, and calculating than teaching religion. These secular subjects were to be taught with great care. "Have you taught those under your guidance the other matters which form part of your duty, such as reading, writing and all the rest, with all possible earnestness?" By providing a full education to their charges, the teachers in the Christian School demonstrated the essential integrity of a complete Christian education. Catechesis, understood in its limited form as the instruction of Christian truths, was not the goal of the Christian Schools. The goal of the Christian Schools was to produce mature, educated Christians—catechesis in the most comprehensive sense—and this entailed more than instruction in the Christian truths, as important as this was. A total Christian education was something that only a school-wide approach could accomplish.

In his text on politeness, De La Salle notes that it is in one's daily relationships that Christian perfection may be found. The point of civility or good manners is to be "guided by the spirit of Jesus Christ. . . . It is this Spirit alone . . . which should inspire all our actions, making them holy and agreeable to God." The respect shown to others, including the poor, is due to a recognition of the fact that they belong to Jesus Christ and are children of God.

The Christian School was a place where students were expected to learn both what they needed to know for immortal salvation and what they needed to know for their mature integration into society as Christian adults. The Brothers were not individuals who taught religion to students. They were not catechists, understood again in the limited sense as those who teach only religious truths. The duties of the teachers included everything from keeping an eye on the students' home life to showing them how to hold a pen, from making sure everyone had something for breakfast to administering corrections for wrongful behavior, from knowing what went on in the streets where students lived to knowing which students would profit by being promoted. As much as the Brothers came to know their students in a variety of situations, the students also came to know their teachers through a variety of school subjects. Such a relationship as De La Salle advocated was one that became established over a period of time through a variety of activities. It was this *relationship* that drew students to the practice of their faith, as well as the particular religious teaching that came from the mouths of their teachers. The combination of firmness and gentleness, methodology and relationship, teaching and example, applied to all the subjects taught in the school and pervading all aspects of school life, was the vehicle for Christian instruction.

As the total life outside the school, with all its manifestations inside of the classroom, was always part of the students, continuous and inseparable from their character, so also the total life inside the school, with all its subjects and concerns *vis-à-vis* life outside, was always part of the teachers and their true ministry as teachers.

♥

5

De La Salle's Vision and Practice Today

It need hardly be said that this is not seventeenth-century France and that De La Salle could not have foreseen the kinds of situations schools of today encounter on a daily basis. Mass media, technology, modern transportation, and secular society are major factors that schools of today take for granted. Add to that compulsory public education, liability lawsuits, and economic necessities—it all adds up to a picture of the Lasallian school that is about as far removed from its namesake in the seventeenth-century as a candle is from a light bulb. Yet the light remains.

To do justice to De La Salle's charism in the contemporary world, one must do justice both to the nature of that charism and to the nature of the contemporary world, placing them in critical dialogue with each other. Having presented De La Salle's own story and the vision and practice that resulted from it, the challenging task of articulating what that vision and practice look like today remains. The best way to do this is to use the language, images, and categories that people relate to today. And the language of today, when it comes to topics such as this, is the language of spirituality.

When people ask "What does it mean to be Lasallian today?" another way of stating it would be "What sort of spirituality is a Lasallian spirituality, and how can it be lived in the schools?"

THE NATURE OF SPIRITUALITY

Before launching into a description of Lasallian spirituality, it would be wise to take a quick look at the nature of spirituality itself. As a matter of fact, the phrase *Lasallian spirituality* is more frequently used than it is understood. Ask any Lasallian educator what Lasallian spirituality means and you will hear opinions ranging from confused platitudes to genuine insight. Each person's experience seems to be different from another's. If the phrase is to have any meaning at all, such meaning will come from the heritage that takes the adjective *Lasallian* as its own.

Today, in the United States, the word *spirituality* is used to describe the totality of an essentially personal experience involving a variety of integrated dimensions. Astronauts and journalists, New Age ministers and taxicab drivers, government officials and Lasallian educators all seem to be reaching for a comprehensive consideration of their daily experience when they use this term.

The history of the use of the word *spirituality* does not provide much help in defining its meaning for today. One theologian, Sandra Schneiders, brings some clarity to the issue by saying that the study of Christian spirituality is a field whose object is the Christian spiritual life as experience and whose methodology includes description, analysis, and constructive interpretation so as to fully understand it. (In that sense, Lasallian spirituality deals with the description, analysis, and constructive interpretation of the experience found in a Lasallian setting.) For most people, however, the word *spirituality* simply refers to any wide-ranging, marginally understood, deeply personal sense of integrity and purpose. It is the word that is used when all other words aren't big enough or deep enough.

To find what the word means for De La Salle and his story, one must take the word *spirituality* seriously and look at how the Holy Spirit's effective presence in De La Salle's life defined it for him. When we look at De La Salle's lifelong encounter with God in the world, what description of that experience emerges?

De La Salle himself provided a key to his spiritual journey when he said that God led him "in an imperceptible way and over a long period of time so that one commitment led to another in a way that I did not foresee in the beginning." From 1679 on, De La Salle found himself drawn into ever deepening convictions, ever widening commitments, and ever more challenging practices. As his convictions grew, so did his commitments and so did his practices. Together, these formed the living reality that constitutes his unique charism, his living spirituality. De La Salle's essential integrity, the continuity of his reflected experience, shaped the nature of his spirituality. Who he was defined what he would do.

De La Salle's personal integrity shaped the character of what *spirituality* means within a Lasallian context: spirituality refers to the dynamic integration of foundational convictions, basic operative commitments, and consistent practices. This definition of the word "spirituality," like all definitions, is universally accessible and could be applied to situations other than De La Salle's. But since it emerges particularly from De La Salle's personal spiritual experience, it is particularly applicable to him and to his charism. In De La Salle's life, what stands out is the degree to which the integrity between faith-filled convictions, commitments, and practices became manifest.

THE NATURE OF LASALLIAN SPIRITUALITY

When one looks at the *Lasallian* part of Lasallian spirituality, two things are immediately evident. These are two things that anyone who has read the previous sections of this book will quickly recognize: (1) Lasallian spirituality is intimately associated with Lasallian pedagogy, and (2) Christ's life lies at the heart of Lasallian spirituality.

1. Lasallian spirituality is a spirituality that has the school as its setting, the teacher as its focus, and the salvific potential of education as its inspiration. De La Salle's writings show that the Lasallian educator's life with his or her students constitutes the very center his or her religious experience. For the Lasallian educator, the school is the privileged place where God is to be encountered.

There is no separation between the professional journey and the spiritual journey. Both are aspects of a single vocation and commitment to education. Likewise, Lasallian pedagogy is Lasallian precisely *because of, not in spite of or along with,* its spiritual dimensions. Educational historians credit De La Salle with many educational innovations, but not one of these historians has yet pointed out that it is ultimately the life of faith that motivated and shaped the pedagogy of De La Salle and his Brothers. His spirituality is focused on the specific approach, implementation, and context of the activity of education. And the way he came to describe that spirit[uality] was in terms of faith and zeal, a single spirit consisting of two parts that are intimately related to one another. Both come to fruition in the ministry of teaching and the work of education.

2. The life of Christ lying at the core of De La Salle's commitments also lies at the core of Lasallian spirituality. Despite many aspects of seventeenth-century French spirituality that would find little favor today, "the Christocentric spirituality of the French School was diffused so widely that for all practical purposes Catholic spirituality in modern times could be characterized as French spirituality." (Aumann, 1985, p. 218)

Christ is to be found in the teacher: "you are ambassadors and ministers of Christ . . . representing Christ himself. He wants your disciples to see him in you and receive your instructions as if he were giving them to them." Lasallian educators have been chosen to be "cooperators in the salvation of souls," precursors of Christ, even apostles. They make Jesus Christ a reality in the lives of their students.

Christ is to be found in the student: "Recognize Jesus [in] . . . the children whom you have to instruct. Adore him in them." Would it make a difference, do you think, if teachers treated their students as "living images of Jesus Christ" and "as children of God himself"? De La Salle calls each soul a living plant in the field of the church, the Body of Christ, a soul for which the educator is responsible.

Christ is to be found in the work of education: the task is "to help your disciples to save themselves . . . you must lead them to unite all their actions to those of Jesus Christ." The work of salvation, the proclamation of the Gospel, is truly encountered and practically enacted in the day-to-day activities, relationships, and realities that make up school life. The goal is nothing less than "to establish and maintain the reign of God in the hearts of your students."

faith

zeal

community

Christ is to be found in the prayer of education: "Constantly represent the needs of your disciples to Jesus Christ, explaining to him the difficulties you experience in guiding them." Prayer obtains all that one needs for effective teaching, drawing "upon yourself the light you must have to know how to form Jesus Christ in the hearts of the children entrusted to your guidance."

TEN LASALLIAN OPERATIVE COMMITMENTS

Bearing in mind the definition of *spirituality* that comes from De La Salle's own spiritual experience (the dynamic integration of foundational convictions, basic operative commitments, and consistent practices), we can best describe that spirituality as a set of basic operative commitments that turn convictions into practices, that integrate faith and zeal. These commitments are postures, orientations, intentionalities that make people decide to do one thing instead of another, to go here instead of there, to deal with this situation instead of that one. The language of commitments is appropriate because they can be described, they can be seen in action, and they speak to the hundreds of daily decisions that make up an educator's day.

The ten basic operative commitments of Lasallian spirituality that have been chosen emerge out of the Lasallian tradition itself, being based on dimensions of Lasallian life that have been continuously upheld throughout its three-hundred-year history. They are explicit, focused, intentional commitments each of which meets the following criteria:

- based on events in the life of John Baptist de La Salle
- supported by foundational convictions in his writings
- evident as operative commitments in early Lasallian history
- reflected in consistent practices within Lasallian schools
- meaningful for the contemporary situation of schools and society
- impossible to imagine *not* finding in a school in the Lasallian tradition

- possible to imagine a school in a different tradition as functioning successfully without; i.e., giving emphasis where none is generally assumed

As with all commitments, these ten Lasallian operative commitments express directions; they provide an operative structure by which fidelity may be measured. They are presented in the form of attributes, qualities that identify the specific commitments of Lasallian character. As such, they become operative when joined with particular activities. Remember that they are components of a *dynamic* reality.

The first set of five commitments are more directly related to the spirit of faith; they speak of inner dynamics of Lasallian pedagogical spirituality. The second set of five commitments are more directly related to the spirit of zeal; they speak of exterior dynamics of Lasallian pedagogical spirituality, ones that effectively color the mission flowing from Lasallian identity.

The Spirit of Faith

- *Centered in and nurtured by the life of faith.* Christian faith provides the motivation, the context, the direction, and the support for the mission of Lasallian education.
- *Trusting Providence in discerning God's will.* God guides those engaged in the Lasallian mission with absolute trustworthiness. The work is God's; we are but God's instruments.
- *With creativity and fortitude.* When the invitation to the Lasallian mission is clear, God blesses and supports that which is done with imagination and determination, ingenuity and endurance.
- *Through the agency of the Holy Spirit.* The Spirit of Christ affects the work of salvation through prayerful persons open to God's dynamic presence both within their souls and in expressing their Lasallian mission.
- *Incarnating Christian paradigms and dynamics.* The Lasallian mission brings alive and brings present Gospel

realities and the essential elements of Christian life within the world of education.

The Spirit of Zeal

- *With practical orientation.* Lasallian education strives to be realistic in its approach, its ends, and its goals. Prayer is put to work; practicality counts.
- *Devoted to accessible and comprehensive education.* Lasallian education must be accessible to all who desire it, and it must include all that constitutes a complete Christian education.
- *Committed to the poor.* Lasallian education makes every effort to be of service to the poor, to make educational service of the poor an effective priority.
- *Working in association.* Lasallian education is accomplished as a common dedication to the church-wide mission of education, one marked by cooperation, collaboration, and complementarity.
- *Expressing a lay vocation.* Lasallian education is a lay vocation expressing, enlivening, and encouraging common baptismal realities as followers of Jesus Christ.

RATIONALE AND CONSEQUENCES

A first reading of these ten commitments will not cause most people to become very excited. After all, aren't these commitments ones that are found in all sorts of other places? In fact, some of them are things that we should be doing as Christians whether we're at a Lasallian school or not. Wouldn't this list look pretty much the same if it referred to a school run by Dominicans, or Franciscans, or Jesuits, or Benedictines, or dedicated lay people?

The short answer is no. The long answer is maybe. What must be remembered is that Christian life is not split up into discrete little units that each have their own character. We're dealing with a living reality here; a reality that has a *dynamic presence* at work in its midst, the Holy Spirit. Education within that reality will always be of a certain kind if it is to remain authentic to its source. Hence, Lasallian education must always be

friendship

prayer

teaching

Christian education and, as such, will be the same as any other authentic Christian education. Where the differences lie is in the particulars. "God is in the details" said Mies van der Rohe, a German architect. This is as true here as it is in the blueprint of a building. God is not a God of generalities, but a God of details—real people encountering the practicalities of real situations with real intentionalities.

Take jazz piano as an example. One pianist can take a tune and do an improvisation on it that immediately identifies his or her style. Another pianist can take the same tune and make it sound entirely different by choosing to play a different set of notes in a different way. Yet both pianists have only the eighty-eight keys to choose from and only the one tune to work with. The difference lies in the particulars, not in the tune. Similarly, the tune that Lasallian education plays is the same as that of other Catholic schools, but the particulars for how that tune is played can vary rather significantly. There may be only so many commitments that those of us in education can choose from. Yet the ones chosen here are the ones that for us, in this combination, with these particular emphases, give the tune of Catholic Christian education a Lasallian personality.

To understand how each Lasallian operative commitment fits into the life of a school, they will be looked at more closely in two groups. The first set of five commitments, those that express inner dynamics flowing from the spirit of faith, will be considered together in terms of their rationale and their application as applied to five components of an educational institution—the student, the teacher, the teacher-student relationship, the activity of teaching, and the school in general. The second set of five commitments, those that express the external dynamics flowing from the spirit of zeal, will then be considered together in the same way. Along with each commitment, a number of related quotations from De La Salle and from other sources will be provided, and each short section will conclude with several questions for personal reflection and follow-up.

FIVE COMMITMENTS RELATED TO THE SPIRIT OF FAITH

Centered in and Nurtured by the Life of Faith:

Perhaps more often than not, we tend to overlook the most obvious things. We notice what it means to live in the United States when we travel outside of the country; we notice our cultural / social position when we are placed in a radically different one; and we appreciate our deeper commitments to things when we find those commitments tested at inconvenient times. In the world of Lasallian education, the most obvious—and most easily overlooked—piece of the picture is the fact of faith; profound, deep, all-encompassing, vibrant faith.

What else but faith drove the young De La Salle to heed the words of Scripture, the needs of society, and the momentum of circumstances to take up the thankless, demanding, messy business of organizing marginally competent teachers for schools as poor and forgotten as the families they served? What else but faith fed his persistence in that work when all human indications urged him to abandon it? What else but faith led him for forty years to spend his time, energies, intellect, and personal charism with individuals that in the society of his time were considered, at best, a workforce for the privileged class.

When you consider the prevalent societal notions in 17th century France, even given the vast charitable projects undertaken by many people, De La Salle stands out as someone who held the demands of faith higher than the demands of society. Where society insisted on class distinctions, De La Salle broke those distinctions by his admissions policies and class seating arrangements. Where society established strong educational limitations based on status, privilege, and connections, De La Salle kept his teachers tightly focused on the needs of the students. Where society provided education for the poor in order to keep them under control and prepare them to enter society's workforce, De La Salle provided education as a means of liberating the poor, providing them with some measure of control over their own future in society. Where society saw things through its own lens, De La Salle had only the open eyes of faith.

Such a pervasive faith cannot be sustained unless it is combined with a vigorous life of prayer; not only the on-your-knees profoundly devotional kind of prayer, but also the at-your-side profoundly relational kind of prayer. If De La Salle placed a pebble on the place where his arms rested on the kneeler in his room so that when his head dropped down during prayer for lack of sleep he would instantly be re-awakened, he also wrote thousands of individual monthly letters to his followers, giving advice, urging them on, and sharing in their specific responsibilities. A realistice lived-out faith was always, and is always, job one.

In a contemporary environment filled with tremendous societal pressures, uncompromising scientific paradigms, largely therapeutic models of behavior, and a technological televisual culture that permits transcendence only if it is couched in the miraculous, the innocuous, or the pharmacological, can we still bring true "salvation" to the young, especially the poor, by providing an education that is centered in and nurtured by the life of faith? The untamed particularity of personhood that forces us to see the depths of mystery in one another tells us again and again that not only can it be done, it must be done. But it is a task that can only succeed if it is itself centered in and nurtured by the life of faith.

De La Salle's first concern in all that he did, whether for himself, for the teachers, or for the Christian School, was the life of faith, the reality of God's saving presence in Jesus Christ. There was simply nothing else that finally merited his attention. The faith that had grown rich and deeply rooted with age was a faith made strong through exertion and adversity. This same penetrating realization of faith became the core and the support of the Institute that De La Salle founded, the spirit that established the schools' integrating orientation and defined their dynamic identity.

Consequences for taking such a commitment seriously: **students** would gradually discern and appreciate God's living presence through both curricular requirements and extra curricular activities; **teachers** would introduce the paradigm of God's saving grace to students by modeling and fostering the knowledge, skills, and dispositions needed for Christian maturity in today's society; the **teacher-student relationship** would live out God's compassionate concern for the total welfare of a particular student in a particular situation; the **activity of teaching** would usher students towards Christian maturity by demonstrating and pursuing that maturity;

and **the school** would initiate, demonstrate, and support a realistically rendered life of faith through its structures and organizational dynamics.

From De La Salle's Writings:

Be convinced that you will contribute to the good of the Church . . . only insofar as you have the fullness of faith and are guided by the spirit of faith.
(De La Salle –Meditations 139.2)

The main purpose of faith is to lead us to practice what we believe. . . . Be convinced that the main conversion is that of the heart and without it the conversion of the mind is quite sterile. (De La Salle – *Meditations* 175.2)

It is in vain that you believe what Jesus Christ proposed to you in the holy Gospel if your actions do not give proof of your belief; in such a case your faith is in vain [James 2:20]. . . . How do you show that you possess the spirit of Christianity? Be assured that to possess it your actions must not give the lie to the faith you profess, but rather be a lively expression of what is written in the Gospel.
(De La Salle – *Meditations* 84.3)

Faith and charity; it is these two virtues which make us true Christians. Without them we can neither lead a Christian life nor be agreeable to God, nor even be happy. In fact, what a Christian needs to do in this world is to know God and to love Him. In this all his duties are summed up. We know God by faith, and charity makes us love Him. (De La Salle – *Duties of a Christian* – Preface)

From Institute Documents:

More than in any other domain, education to freedom is required when there is a question of instruction in the faith. The Christian school should be the freest of institutions; it suggests without coercion the infinite possibilities of life according to Christ; it announces the good news of the Gospel to each one insofar as [she or] he is ready for it, and with absolute respect for the freedom of all. (*Declaration*, 46.4)

In response to the design of God in his regard, St. John Baptist de La Salle transformed his entire life into a spiritual journey of ever increasing faith.
(1987 *Rule*, Article 8)

Personal Follow-up Questions:

1) How do I sustain my faith-life? (Do I have a faith-life?)

2) In my way of approaching life, do I look upon everything with the eyes of faith, do everything in view of God, and attribute all to God?

3) What specific, small thing could I do that would feed my faith?

Trusting Providence in Discerning God's Will:

It would be hard for us to imagine the degree to which John Baptist de La Salle trusted in God's continual, loving care, and how much this providential sensitivity shaped the educational enterprise that he undertook. His deepest conviction and consistent prayer was "Domine, opus tuum." [Lord, the work is yours.]

De La Salle lived his entire adult life in faithful surrender to the designs of God's Providence. This surrender increasingly became a conscious, continual decision on his part. The circumstances that he encountered each day manifested God's grace to him, bearing God's loving concern and communicating God's will. In this respect, his attitude was not unlike that of Mother Teresa, who, during a trip around the United States, was told each morning about the day's delays, problems, and changes by her traveling companion. She finally said: "These should not be seen as problems. We must look on them as God's gifts to us." (Of course, the next day her traveling companion told her: "Mother, this morning God gave us a very big gift. . . .") De La Salle's attitude was very similar to Mother Teresa's. When God is in the picture, God *is* the picture.

This, however, does not mean that De La Salle was passive or submissive about the ways of the world. In one letter he writes, "Don't let slip opportunities that come your way, but don't be overeager." God remains in the lead: "I don't like to make the first move in any endeavor. . . . I leave it to Divine Providence to make the first move and then I am satisfied." Virtually every educational project that he undertook was a practical response to a direct request from an individual or representative group. The Gospel came to life through real educational needs, real educational situations, and real educational responses. Instead of making a virtue out of necessity, De La Salle found virtue through necessity.

De La Salle came to know that what God ultimately wanted, including possible failure, was the basic good. "If my work does not come from God, I would consent to its ruin. I would join our enemies in destroying it if I thought that it did not have God for its author, or that he did not will its progress." The work of Christian education would succeed insofar as it depended on God's Providence.

association

education

reflection

The schools themselves reflected God's radical providential care toward each one of the students, many of whom often had experienced little care in their lives. De La Salle's profound dependence on the graces hidden in day-to-day circumstances led to schools where young people could depend on teachers who shared such hidden graces in their day-to-day ministry.

In a contemporary world where the ideal of self-sufficiency appears to outweigh any radical reliance on God's providence, the challenge of educators is to balance a good sense of self with a real sensitivity to God's loving voice—experienced in reflection, circumstances, and even suffering. When you pay attention to the voice of providence in your life, you cannot but exclaim: "My God! It's been you all the time." Then discernment becomes a real possibility, God is revealed as a trustworthy friend or loving parent, and life bursts out all over with grace.

Consequences for taking such a commitment seriously: **students** would pursue an appreciation for God's designs in their lives and in the life of the world through cultivating habits of pursuing the complexity and mysterious nature of the world; **teachers** would seek God's providential guidance through struggling with common educational challenges, delving into reality's hidden depths, and uncovering humanity's capacity for goodness; the **teacher-student relationship** would cooperate with God's providential guidance in the lives of students by paying true attention to individual students and their experienced lives; the **activity of teaching** would itself play out like an improvised experiential fugue, with lines of inquiry fluid throughout; and **the school** would move from one commitment to the next, without hurry or compulsiveness.

From De La Salle's Writings:

When a person abandons himself to the Providence of God it is like a man who puts himself out to the high sea without either sails or oars.
(De La Salle – Meditations 134.1)

Be convinced that if you truly seek the kingdom of God and his justice, all these things will be given to you besides [Mt. 6:33], because it is God himself who takes responsibility for the care to provide for you. . . . The more you abandon yourselves to God for what concerns your temporal needs, the more care he will take to provide for you. (De La Salle – *Meditations* 67.3)

As for myself, I do not like to make the first move in any endeavor, and I will not do it in Rome any more than elsewhere. I leave it to Divine Providence to make the first move and then I am satisfied. When it is clear that I am acting only under the direction of Providence, I have nothing to reproach myself with. When I make the first move, it is only I myself who am active, so I don't expect to see much good result; neither does God usually give the action his special blessing. (De La Salle – *Letter 18*)

I know it is better to live in more difficult circumstances, withdrawn from worldly concerns, and I am glad that you are in such dispositions. Still, when you decide to do this, you must put yourself entirely in the hands of Divine Providence, or, if you have not enough virtue for that nor enough faith, then you must take the necessary means before you carry out your plan. If you do neither, you are not acting as a Christian nor as an intelligent man. (De La Salle – *Letter 19*)

From Institute Documents:

The spirit of this Institute is first, a spirit of faith, which should induce those who compose it not to look upon anything but with the eyes of faith, not to do anything but in view of God, and to attribute all to God, always entering into these sentiments of Job: "The Lord gave and the Lord has taken away; as it has pleased the Lord, so it is done", and into other similar sentiments so often expressed in Holy Scripture and uttered by the Patriarchs of old. (1718 *Rule*)

John Baptist de La Salle was deeply moved by the way in which "the children of the artisans and the poor" were abandoned and left to themselves. As a practical response to his prayerful consideration of this fact in relation to God's plan of salvation, he came to discern, in faith, what God wanted the mission of the Institute to be. (1987 *Rule,* Article 11)

Personal Follow-up Questions:

1) When did you last spend more than 30 seconds thinking about what God is doing with you?

2) How can you discover God's will for your school? Where are the signs?

3) Are you a means of God's providential care for someone else? How seriously do you take it?

<u>With Creativity and Fortitude:</u>
What is often forgotten in many discussions about De La Salle is the tremendous amount of creativity he applied to turning his educational vision into a reality. Hand in hand with that creativity went a fortitude, a courage, that moved his work forward in bold strokes. It was through bold, persistent innovation that De La Salle and the Brothers succeeded where so many others had failed. Numerous examples from the early history of the Institute illustrate the point.

This "life theme" in De La Salle became established when he gave up his inheritance and his honored position at the Cathedral of Reims in order to throw his lot in with the would-be schoolmasters. During the famine of 1683-84, De La Salle distributed his fortune (over $400,000) as bread for the poor and resigned his canonry at the Cathedral. This move demonstrated both his solidarity with his followers and his radical dependence on God's providential care. Instead of endowing the schools—an obvious move to his followers—he went much deeper. In contrast with their own commitment, his commitment to this new enterprise must have been quite an example to his young followers.

In the same way, some years later when Brothers were literally dying from overwork, others were leaving after having been trained as teachers, and various pastors or bishops were trying to take control of their future, De La Salle make a couple of creative, bold moves. He took an "heroic vow" with two other Brothers to ensure that the group would become established "even if we have to beg for alms and to live on bread alone." He found a house in the country where his followers could be trained and could come to on retreat or to relax. And he called everyone together for an extensive spiritual retreat, rekindling the fire of their commitment and instituting a system of monthly correspondence so that he might continue to build up their strength and guide their spiritual lives.

In the schools, this same creativity and fortitude operated. The handbook for schools that De La Salle and the Brothers created includes innovative methods for teaching French, reading, handwriting, mathematics, and religion. De La Salle's first book for the schools was *Teaching French Syllables* which, in effect, eventually standardized French pronunciation throughout the country. The book from which students learned to read was a politeness book, written in the kind of script they would encounter in the job market, so that their manners would improve along with their reading skill. Religious education included the singing of popular tunes of the day, but with lyrics based on the catechism lessons, and several books concerning one's behavior in church were written. A personalized record was kept for each student which talked about his strengths and weaknesses, his family relationships, and the approaches that worked best. This record was passed on to other teachers so that they could work with that student more effectively. On every level, the student was the central concern; new teaching methods or resources were devised and implemented for the sake of the student.

This subtle combination of creativity and fortitude and "that 'unruffled boldness' of the Founder's can be explained in the last analysis, only by the spiritual quality and the genuine holiness of his life, for his only ambition was at all times and despite all obstacles to adhere, in view of faith, to God's will clearly known, and to the designs of Providence." (Rayez, 1952, p. 4). The foundations in Reims, Paris, Avignon, Rouen, and many others began with tentative steps, gradually growing into major ventures that were by no means secure but that were nevertheless persistent despite many obstacles. During De La Salle's lifetime, almost sixty schools were established all over France. Of these, not more than about forty were still open and staffed by his teachers at the time of his death. De La Salle and his followers responded to the needs around them by opening and closing schools according to the designs of Providence. This boldness was based on the conviction that God works through us and through our creativity. When we are creative in responding to what we know needs to be done, and as we act on that creativity with conviction and fortitude, we share in God's life in our midst and make St. John Baptist De La Salle's attitude our own.

Consequences for taking such a commitment seriously: **students** would cultivate a natural boldness, a sense of adventure, and the power of the imagination, gradually discovering in the presence of God a deep and constant source of creativity and fortitude; **teachers** would demonstrate resourcefulness and resilience, imagination and determination, ingenuity and persistence as redeeming and liberating dynamics; the **teacher-student relationship** would anchor and shape the shifting whirlwind of newly discovered relational capacities through a combination of empathy and detachment, individual application and common accountability; the **activity of teaching** would pursue innovative methodologies and engaging curricula with persistent determination; and **the school** would creatively enact, without apology, its Christian dimensions and would resolutely pursue them.

From De La Salle's Writings:

[The students] must understand what you say, so you must give them instructions adapted to their capacity; otherwise what you say would be of little use. (De La Salle – *Meditations* 33.3)

[O]ne of the main concerns of those who instruct others: to be able to understand their students and to discern the right way to guide them. . . . This guidance requires understanding and discernment of spirit. (De La Salle – *Meditations* 33.1)

God diffuses the fragrance of His knowledge throughout the world by human ministers. Just as He commanded light to shine out of darkness, so He also kindles a light in the hearts of those whom He has called to announce His word to children, to enlighten them by making the glory of God known to them.

    Since God in His mercy has given you such a ministry, do not falsify His word but gain glory before Him by proclaiming His truth to those whom you are called to teach. Let this be your continual effort in the lessons you give them, looking upon yourselves as the ministers of God and the administrators of His mysteries. (De La Salle – *Meditations,* 193.1)

This guide has been prepared and put in order (by the late M. De La Salle) only after a great number of conferences between him and the oldest Brothers of the Institute and those most capable of running a school well, and after several years of experience. Nothing has been added that has not been thoroughly deliberated and well tested, nothing of which the advantages and disadvantages have not been weighed and, as far as possible, of which the good or bad consequences have not been foreseen. (The *Conduct,* Preface)

From Other Sources:

La Salle was an innovator in response, not to an intuition, but to the requests and needs of others. Ramification in the work of the Brothers did not come from innate charism but from sensitivity and openness to the educational needs of the population around them. (Calcutt, *De La Salle,* p. 423)

There is a need for both individual and community effort, based on creative study, to discover new and adapted forms of education to meet the needs of those among the poor who are most neglected. . . . It is of the utmost importance that from the center to every part of the Institute there be a bold and generous response to the immense suffering of people in the world today. (*Declaration*, 33.1, 33.4)

The Brothers [and others] bear witness to their love for St. John Baptist de La Salle as their Founder. They imitate him in his abandonment to God, his loyalty to the Church, his creative apostolic spirit, and his definitive commitment to the evangelization of young people. The life of an Institute is a continual challenge to be creative while remaining faithful to its origins. (1987 *Rule*, Article 149)

Personal Follow-up Questions:

1) How are you creative and bold in the policies and practices that you influence?

2) What would make you sensitive to innovations occuring in your midst?

3) Where could you be more courageous in what you do?

Through the Agency the Holy Spirit:

What comes to mind when you think about the Holy Spirit? More than likely your mind flashes on the visual image of a hovering dove, perhaps with a small halo around its head as if in a Renaissance painting. If pushed a little further, you might say that the Holy Spirit is a member of the Trinity and involved with various charismatic movements in the church. Somehow, however, the Holy Spirit remains a bit of a mystery, removed from everyday life, the subject of theological speculation.

For De La Salle, the Holy Spirit was as real and alive as the kids that were encountered in the classroom each day. It was because of the Spirit of Jesus, the Spirit of God, that he had become involved in this work in the first place, and it was the dynamic presence of the Spirit in the teaching encounter that transformed it into a means of salvation for both the students and the teacher. Teaching became a gospel ministry through the life of the Holy Spirit.

The entire bulk of apostolic activity, all the grinding details of an educational life, were means of entering more fully into the life of the Spirit. Good example, Gospel maxims, daily contact, continual vigilance, frequent prayer, and comprehensive formation—all accentuate the active role that the Holy Spirit had in establishing the

Christian Schools and in sustaining their charismatic effectiveness. De La Salle came to appreciate in deep and concrete ways the actions of the Holy Spirit within the Body of Christ, the church. "Docility to the Spirit of Christ is beyond any doubt whatsoever truly central in Lasallian spirituality" (Laube, 1970, p. 224).

Seventeenth century French spirituality recognized that the Holy Spirit played a central role in all of Christian life. One's daily life became more "Christian" to the extent that the Spirit of Jesus shaped one's interior dispositions. The Christian incarnates the very being of Jesus through the actions and attitudes of his or her life. The more that the Christian becomes engaged in good works with an attitude like that of Jesus, the more the Spirit of Jesus, the Holy Spirit, comes alive in the process and advances the work of the church, which is itself the mystical body of Jesus that is an active and present reality in the world today because of the vitality of that same Holy Spirit.

The key elements in this process are the actions we take, the attitudes we have, and the articulations that we make. De La Salle urged his teachers to constantly pray for their students, bring all their daily teaching concerns to God, and ask that the Spirit of Jesus come alive in them and in their work in the classroom. He also told his teachers that their attitude should be Christ's, that they should see Jesus in their students and look upon them as Jesus would. All their most important and effective actions will flow from their prayer life and from their deliberate effort to take on the dispositions of Jesus.

When we take Jesus seriously and enter into the dynamic mystery of God's life in our midst, we discover that the Spirit of Jesus, the Holy Spirit, bursts forth with unexpected strength and abundant grace. Approaching a situation with the dispositions of Jesus and moving forward in deliberate action based on those dispositions brings God's dynamic into play, and suddenly we find more than we had any right to expect. This is the life of the Holy Spirit and one central reason why De La Salle's approach to education is consistently more dynamic, more desired, and more demanding that most of us may realize.

Consequences for taking such a commitment seriously: **students** would find the Spirit working in their lives through continual, ap-

service

learning

together

propriately nuanced introductions of specific connections, challenges, and realization of Christian sensibility, especially service of others; **teachers,** as animators of Christ's life in the school, would be shaped by regular interior prayer, diligent personal study, and habitual times of retreat; the **teacher-student relationship** would bring to expression the movement of God's love established in one's soul; the **activity of teaching** would enkindle the Spirit in students' hearts through the knowledge, love, and passion with which particular subjects are taught; and **the school** would maintain the unity of mind and heart that characterizes the Spirit's presence in community through making explicit and present the implicit, hidden substance of the school's apostolic mission.

From De La Salle's Writings:

In order for you to fulfill this duty with as much perfection and exactness as God requires of you, frequently give yourselves to the Spirit of our Lord to act in your work only under his influence, so that your own spirit may have no part in it. This Holy Spirit, then, will come upon them generously, so that they will be able to possess fully the Christian spirit. (De La Salle – *Meditations,* 195.2)

The more your work for the good of your disciples is given life by him and draws its power from him, the more it will produce good in them. This is why you must ask him earnestly that all your instructions be given life by his Spirit and draw all their power from him. [He] . . . is the one who enlightens the minds of your students and leads them to love and to practice the good that you teach them.
(De La Salle – *Meditations,* 195.3)

The truths which the Holy Spirit teaches to those who receive him are the maxims found in the holy Gospel. He helps them to understand these maxims and to take them to heart, and he leads them to live and act in accordance with them.

For the Spirit of God alone can give us a correct understanding of these maxims of the Gospel and can inspire us to put them into practice, because they are above the level of the human spirit. How, indeed, can we ever realize that blessed are the poor, that we should love those who hate us, and rejoice when we are calumniated and when people say all sorts of evil against us, that we should return good for evil, and so many other truths entirely contrary to what nature suggests, unless the Spirit of God himself teaches them to us?

You are obliged to teach these holy maxims to the children you are charged to instruct. You must be thoroughly convinced of them yourself, so that you may impress them deeply on the hearts of your pupils. Make yourself docile, therefore, to the Holy Spirit, who can in a short time procure for you a perfect understanding of these truths. (De La Salle – *Meditations,* 44.2)

In all we do for the glory of God and the salvation of souls, we should undertake
nothing without praying to ask God for the light and grace we need to succeed in
whatever we undertake for him in this holy ministry, which can succeed only insofar as we are aided by his help and directed by his Holy Spirit.
(De La Salle – *Meditations*, 107.1))

From Institute Documents:

[Lasallian educators] are convinced that in the life, work, and writings of Saint John
Baptist de La Salle, the Holy Spirit is revealed in a privileged manner, and that they
will find there even today a living principle for their guidance. (*Declaration*, 5.1)

By a spirit of prayer and an attentiveness to the presence of God, [Lasallian educators]
remain sensitive to the guidance of the Holy Spirit, who leads them to an ever deeper appreciation of the realities of faith. (1987 *Rule*, Article 6)

Personal Follow-up Questions:

1) How is the Holy Spirit part of your life? Do you ever think
   about it?

2) What parts of the school's life would benefit from an awareness
   of the Holy Spirit's agency?

3) Where in the school's structure could the Spirit of Jesus find a
   particular opportunity to have an influence?

Incarnating Christian Paradigms and Dynamics:

A school in the Lasallian tradition cannot be separated from a
school in the Christian tradition. The kind of educational community that characterizes a Lasallian school emerges solely with
reference to the kind of faith community that characterizes the
Body of Christ. Both the context and the substance of what occurs in a Lasallian school on a daily basis arises out of dynamics
and paradigms that have a Christian character.

De La Salle delved into the work of educating the young in order to make the Gospel a reality in their lives. He came to see that
his teachers were to "preach" an alternative way of life, becoming
ambassadors for God's incarnated Word through an incarnation of
Jesus' life within the lives of their students. By example, vigilance,
instruction, care, and a well-organized program of Christian formation, the Gospel would have a chance to take root and those
who were presently "far from salvation" would find it within reach.

The primary task of these Christian Schools ("Catholic Schools" in 17th century French terminology) was to bring the young to understand and enter into the "principal Christian mysteries"—the Trinity, the Incarnation, the Redemption, and so on. In 17th century French spirituality, the Christian makes explicit acts of faith in such mysteries and incarnates the very being of Jesus by adopting actions and interior attitudes similar to those Christ first brought to reality by His every deed, His every feeling, His every outlook—in terms of their depth and effect, His every "mystery." By entering into Christ's dispositions, one enters into Christ's mystical reality of salvation and thereby comes to act, and to be, more and more like Him. Insofar as teachers and students lived out these same dispositions, they were formed into true Christians.

The other task of the Christian Schools was to bring the young into the fullness of life that was their inheritance as children of God. The practical maxims of the Gospel, along with the many details of school life that bore witness to a deliberate, Christian perspective, brought the reality of salvation into the classroom. Concern for "salvation" on the practical level went hand-in-hand with "salvation" on the spiritual level. Students grew into their faith in an environment that by its very nature and methods saturated their school lives with God's life and its engagement.

In contemporary life, where success is seen as a greater prize than faithfulness, a holy life might seem like an anachronism. Yet it is precisely the ends of religious education that best define the experience of those who are content and happy with their lives. A holy life that reaches through the whole of life is what the Gospel describes as "life to the full." The challenge today is to take to heart James Joyce's description of the church—"Here comes everybody!"—and De La Salle's description of the Christian School—"Teach them to lead good lives, by instructing them in the mysteries of our faith and by inspiring them with Christian maxims, and thus give them a suitable education."

Consequences for taking such a commitment seriously: **students** would begin to engage the life of faith through the development of convictions, habits of life, dispositions, and gestures of selflessness; **teachers** would cultivate his or her graced position as a teacher of God's mysteries, finding God's presence in the various minutiae of their ministry; the **teacher-student relationship** would look to the way Jesus dealt with his disciples as the way to deal with their students; the **activity of teaching** would strive to touch the hearts of students with the same loving, persistent, familiar approach exemplified by and through Jesus Christ; and **the school** would make real the daily Christian challenges of faith-filled action, mutual forbearance, and charity.

From De La Salle's Writings:

In His providential care, God . . . sends persons with the necessary enlightenment and zeal to help children attain the knowledge of God and His mysteries. According to the grace of Jesus Christ given to them by God, they are like good master-builders who give all possible care and attention to lay the foundation of religion and Christian virtue in the hearts of these children, many of whom would otherwise be abandoned. (De La Salle – *Meditations* 193.2)

No one knows who God is save the Spirit of God, and it is this Spirit of God who penetrates everything, even the deepest and most hidden mysteries in God . Pray, therefore, the Spirit of God to make known to you the gifts that God has given you, as Saint Paul says, so that you may announce them to those whom you are commissioned to instruct. (De La Salle – *Meditations* 189.1)

It is surprising that most Christians look upon decorum and politeness as merely human and worldly qualities and do not think of raising their minds to any higher views by considering them as virtues that have reference to God, to their neighbor, and to themselves. . . . Children should do these things out of respect for God in whose presence they are . . . to show others those signs of consideration, honor, and respect appropriate to members of Jesus Christ and living temples of God, enlivened by the Holy Spirit. (De La Salle – *Politeness,* Preface)

From Institute Documents:

It is apostolic to awaken in students a serious attitude towards life and the conviction of the greatness of man's destiny; it is apostolic to make it possible for them, with intellectual honesty and responsibility, to experience the autonomy of personal thought; it is apostolic to help the students to use their liberty to overcome their own prejudices, preconceived ideas, social pressures, as well as the pressures that come from disintegration within the human person; it is apostolic to dispose students to use their intelligence and their training in the service of their fellowmen, to open them to others: to teach them how to listen and to try to understand, to trust and love; it is apostolic to instill in students a sense of trustworthiness, brotherhood, and justice. (*Declaration,* 41.2)

By its organizational structure and the climate that it engenders, the Christian school makes catechesis possible. This catechesis should be lively, centered on the person of the student, in touch with life as it is, based on Scripture and the liturgy, attentive to the teaching of the Church, and concerned with an integral presentation of the Christian message. (1987 *Rule,* Article 15a)

Personal Follow-up Questions:

1) How important is it to you that you are a spiritual person, a Christian, a Catholic?

2) What can you do on a regular basis that would make a small initial impact on your life and a large impact on another's life?

3) Where would you look in your school to find Christianity at work?

FIVE COMMITMENTS RELATED TO THE SPIRIT OF ZEAL

With Practical Orientation:

Lasallian education has a passion for the practical, a passion that pays real attention to immediate realities. A teacher could never survive otherwise; a school would fail without it. St. Augustine's advice is also our own: Pray as if everything depends on God and work as if everything depends on you.

De La Salle set the tone in his own life. He was never one to avoid the practical; indeed, he embraced it. De La Salle did not write about educational philosophy, he wrote educational handbooks and textbooks that focused on gospel maxims, the duties of a Christian, and the practical rules of politeness. His Brothers presented "reflections" (personally crafted observations that spoke from the heart to the heart) that brought religious teachings to life in the lives of students. A handbook for running the schools, written in consultation with his teachers, went through 23 editions up to 1903, each edition adapting to new needs and circumstances.

The schools themselves were eminently practical. Written work concentrated on contracts and ledgers, while math skills dealt with the French monetary system. Students who worked during the week were taught mathematics, drafting, and commerce on Sundays. Schools on the seacoast included classes on navigation and seamanship. De La Salle insisted that the schools be well-run and its teachers be well-trained. Everything was done to insure that these poor and working class students would succeed in French society and become mature members of the church.

Such a commitment to the real needs of students was not without its difficulties. One might almost call the first schools "subversive." When the Guild of Writing Masters, in effect, sued the Brothers for teaching writing—and won—De La Salle ignored the judgment and found other ways of teaching writing. When the local bishop in Chartres, a friend of De La Salle's from seminary days, challenged De La Salle's practice of teaching reading by starting with French instead of Latin, De La Salle held his ground, writing a detailed response on why his method was a much more realistic approach. After more than 30 years of labor, when it seemed to De La Salle that he was hurting the success of the schools, he even took himself out of the picture until he was ordered to return by the Brothers. The practical and spiritual welfare of the students entrusted to his care remained the primary focus throughout his life: practical means for practical ends.

This down-to-earth practicality is found today in Lasallian schools throughout the world, from street-kids in Vietnam who are taught to repair motorcycle engines to students throughout the West who are taught to translate book-knowledge into life-knowledge. Within today's shifting family structures and mass media's tendency to dull one's critical posture into uniformly simplistic thinking habits, the Lasallian School pays practical attention to the real relationships between people, the development of a sensible integrity among personal convictions, and a continuity of purpose from the present to the future. It is those practical sensibilities that continue to make this educational enterprise so necessary and so successful.

Consequences for taking such a commitment seriously: **students** would be educated in all that is necessary for salvation in this world and the next, basic knowledge and skills along with habits of virtue and faith; **teachers** would present learning material in such a way that it makes sense; the **teacher-student relationship** would be characterized by the personal witness of the teacher *vis-à-vis* that which is being taught; the **activity of teaching** would continually keep in mind the practical application of the subject matter through pragmatic methodologies, poignant examples, and compelling witnesses; and **the school** would habitually pursue practical ends and means in its programs, structures, and vision.

From De La Salle's Writings:

[Reasons for teaching reading in French]. . . . 2) The French language being the natural one, is incomparably easier to learn than Latin by children who hear the one spoken and not the other. . . . 4) Reading French prepares the way for reading Latin, whereas Latin does not help for French, as experience teaches us. . . . 10) Experience shows that almost all the boys and girls who do not know Latin, who have neither letters nor the use of the Latin tongue . . . are never able to read Latin well, and make a sorry show when they read it. . . . It is therefore quite useless to spend a lot of time teaching people to read well a language they will never use." (De La Salle – Letter to Bishop Godet des Marais)

In order to bring the children whom you instruct to take on the Christian spirit, you must teach them the practical truths of faith in Jesus Christ and the maxims of the holy Gospel with at least as much care as you teach the truths that are purely doctrinal. (De La Salle – *Meditations* 194.3)

It is, then, not enough to procure for children the Christian spirit and teach them the mysteries and doctrines of our religion. You must also teach them the practical maxims that are found throughout the holy Gospel. But since their minds are not yet sufficiently able to understand and practice these maxims by themselves, you must serve as visible angels for them in two ways. First, you must help them understand the maxims as they are set forth in the holy Gospel. Second you must guide their steps along the way that leads them to put these maxims into practice. (De La Salle – *Meditations* 197.2)

We should not be satisfied with making acts of speculative faith alone, i.e. on truths which we merely believe in. We must often make acts of practical faith also, i.e. on the truths which we must practice. (De La Salle – *Duties of a Christian*)

When the students are to assist at Holy Mass during school time, they will leave school in the order of the benches. . . . Teachers will take care that the students do not go too near the walls, the shops, or the gutter. . . . In order that they may more easily see the students and observe how they behave themselves on the way to Holy Mass, teachers will walk on the opposite side of the street from them, the students walking ahead of the line, with their faces sufficiently turned toward their students to be able to see them all. While on the street, teachers will not admonish students . . . but will wait until the next day, just before going to Holy Mass, to correct them. (The *Conduct*, Ch. 8, Art. 11)

From Institute Documents:

The Christian school endeavors through its program of instruction to prepare its students for their professional life, for marriage and its responsibilities, for service to society and the Church. (*Declaration*, 1967, Section 47.3)

Every Lasallian foundation is embodied, together with the local church, in the culture, the language and the life-style of the place where it is located. Such embodiment ought to be accomplished in keeping with the charism proper to the Institute. (1987 *Rule*, Article 18a)

Personal Follow-up Questions:

1) What would it be like to "shadow" a student at your school for an entire day?

2) How would you describe the practical means and ends of your school's programs and vision?

3) Can you think of two examples where you personally practice what you preach?

Devoted to Accessible and Comprehensive Education:

The most immediate image that should spring to mind when we think about or talk about the Lasallian heritage is the ministry of education. When we are asked what is most important about what we do, our answer must be "education, education, education."

De La Salle set the direction for us when he put aside a career in the church for a career with barely literate, marginally competent schoolmasters. Christian schooling now became the means of salvation for both teachers and students, whether through terminal primary schools or other educational ventures; e.g., a school for adolescents, a Sunday school for working youth, a continuation school for the undisciplined, a technical training school for sailors or future sailors, and several short-lived training schools for future teachers. As long as schooling was involved, De La Salle was willing to consider it as part of the ministry of his followers.

Two qualities, however, were to be maintained. First, the schools had to be gratuitous, an education as freely given as the Gospel itself, without compensation of any kind from students or parents. Each student was treated alike in terms of opportunity and treated individually in terms of capacities.

Secondly, the schools prepared students for Christian life within a very particular society. Their education included whatever was necessary for them to be successful in that society and whatever was necessary for them to live as mature Christians. The students' salvation required both religious formation and pragmatic education, both habits of Christian life and skills for success. The Christian Schools provided an accessible education that assumed very little of the students except that they needed to partake in a comprehensive program that addressed the important areas of life, so that when they left the school they would be well prepared to participate in society and in the Church's life.

The scope of this education is shown in three major written works by De La Salle: *The Conduct of Schools* (a practical handbook for the teachers); *The Duties of a Christian* (a practical catechism for students); and *Rules of Christian Politeness* (a practical guide for proper social manners).

Education in the Lasallian heritage pays attention to the heart of all education; i.e., integrated lives in right relationship with reality—which includes the reality of God and the Paschal Mystery.

If education enables one to acquire all the skills and all the knowledge necessary for life in secular society but fails to instill specific habits of charity, personal principles of spiritual life, or a growing wisdom that places one's endeavors within a wider context, then such education will have essentially failed to provide the necessities for life.

The Lasallian School attests to the truth that strength is found in weakness, that the most in need require the greatest access and find in education the maximum benefit. The Lasallian School also affirms the tradition that education consists of more than facts, figures, and skills; education primarily forms a person for maturity, bringing into fulfillment one's graced capacities and enabling the taking on of one's promised heritage as children of God.

Consequences for taking such a commitment seriously: **students** would not be belittled or frustrated by the educational endeavors of the classroom or the accessibility of the school's normal activities; **teachers** would demonstrate a decided preference for direct educational activity and a comprehensive attention to accessible occasions for Christian formation; the **teacher-student relationship** would have a quality and substance that remains singularly fixed on procuring the student's benefit; the **activity of teaching** would be assiduously prepared, thoroughly engaging, and geared to encountering students where they are, plus challenging them to stretch their given capacities; and **the school** would maintain an unrestrictive, balanced admissions policy and an accessible, comprehensive curriculum, disciplinary procedure, consultative process, and administrative protocol.

From De La Salle's Writings:

God is so good that He not only brings us into existence by His act of creation but also desires that all of us come to the knowledge of truth. This truth is God Himself and all that He has willed to reveal to us through Jesus Christ, through His apostles, and through His church. God desires all of us to be taught this knowledge, that our minds may be enlightened by the light of faith.

We cannot be taught the mysteries of our religion unless we have the good fortune to hear about them, and we cannot have this advantage unless someone preaches the word of God. (De La Salle – *Meditations,* 193.1)

Consider that it is only too common for the working class and the poor to allow their children to live on their own, roaming all over as if they had no home, until they are able to be put to some work. These parents have no concern to send their children to school because they are too poor to pay teachers, or else they have to go out to look for work and leave their children to fend for themselves.

The results of this condition are regrettable. These unfortunate children, accustomed to an idle life for many years, have great difficulty when it comes time for them to go to work. In addition, through association with bad companions they learn to commit many sins which later on are very difficult to stop, the bad habits having been contracted over so long a period of time.

God has had the goodness to remedy so great a misfortune by the establishment of the Christian Schools, where the teaching is offered free of charge and entirely for the glory of God, where children are kept all day and learn reading, writing, and their religion. In these schools the children are always kept busy, so that when their parents want them to go to work, they are prepared for employment. (De La Salle – *Meditations* 194.1)

From Institute Documents:

The educational policies of Lasallian institutions are centered on the young, adapted to the times in which they live, and designed to prepare them to take their place in society. These institutions are characterized by the determination to make the means of salvation available to young people through a quality education and by an explicit proclamation of Jesus Christ . . .

[Lasallian educators] consider their professional work as a ministry. They are attentive to each of their students and especially to those most in need. They make themselves available to all in an attitude of brotherly [and sisterly] companionship, helping them to discover, appreciate and assimilate both human and gospel values. They help young people to grow as persons who are called to realize more and more that they are children of God. (1987 *Rule,* Article 13)

The ultimate purpose of the [Lasallian] educational apostolate, for the poor as well as for all, is to communicate the Christian spirit. (*Declaration,* 30.2)

Persons must be the center of educational systems rather than the prestige of some academic curriculum. (*Declaration,* 31.1)

Personal Follow-up Questions:

1) What is the greatest educational need of the students in your school?

2) Are there subtle (and direct) ways that your school is not quite accessible to all?

3) For a comprehensive education of the students, what areas that you directly influence still need attention?

Committed to the Poor:

There are certain issues that are "pivot-points" for Lasallian educators—issues that are important enough to struggle with continually, to talk about at length, and to deal with on many levels. The Lasallian commitment to the poor is one of those issues.

It is a healthy sign that we do so, for our commitment to education of the poor works hand-in-hand with our commitment to the Gospel itself; something that is never complete, something that is both an irritant and a beckoning, our greatest challenge and our greatest legacy. Boards of trustees and administrators in Lasallian schools grapple with its constant demands and display any evidence of it with justifiable pride. This is a commitment that lies at the heart of what we do as Lasallian educators, and therefore we pay a bit more attention than usual when the topic comes up. It is as if the momentum of centuries of tradition swells up beneath us and carries us forward in favor of the poor, the disadvantaged, and the marginalized.

The centrality of this commitment began with De La Salle and the first schools. He was convinced that the poor were the ones who needed schools the most and that those who themselves practiced

Gospel poverty would run the most effective schools for the poor. The first Christian Schools that came about were endowed parish charity schools that operated on a shoestring budget and were most often located in the less desirable parts of town. The teachers survived with meager food, little sleep, much prayer, very demanding work, and a great passion for educating the poor. Everyone was welcome to attend, provided that they were willing to be treated outside of the prevalent societal categories. Schools were tuition-free not only because the Gospel itself was free, but also because everyone thus became equally poor and equally rich. Of primary worth was each student; of predominant value was an education without borders.

Partiality was shown, however. Those with less attractive qualities were to receive the most attention, and those with the least talents were to be especially supported and encouraged. De La Salle was convinced that the poor were the ones who needed Christian Schools the most. A curriculum that combined practical and religious training was specifically designed to help the poor succeed in society. Penmanship, politeness, and prayer were part of the same picture, pieces of the same program. Those who were without and had little hope of even gaining access to society's limited options became vested members of both society and the church by way of an education that held the Gospel as its model and maintained a decided preference for the disadvantaged as its operational benchmark.

Our inclination toward educational service of the poor is an incentive that brings focus to our efforts and choices. Going beyond concern for the poor as a form a charity, our call is to dwell within the world of the poor and to allow that world to define how we respond to all the rest, instead of the other way around. "How can we teach the poor?" becomes "How can the poor teach us?" Such a switch in priorities is neither quick, comfortable, or easy—there are real consequences and real costs. Yet school programs and curricula discover what they seek based on the questions that they pose, and the Lasallian school is one where the commitment to the poor is as real as the poor themselves are.

Consequences for taking such a commitment seriously: **students** would become aware of poverty, its causes, and its social undercurrents through classwork, service projects, insertion programs, and retreats; **teachers** would model a reflective critical stance regarding society's manipulative influences and the lasting riches, deeper fame, and quiet power of fulfilling Christian lives; the **teacher-student relationship** would give particular attention to disadvantaged students without prejudice, hidden or implied; the **activity of teaching** would include successful strategies for overcoming personal and societal limitations; and **the school** would be sensitive to local social needs in terms of its curriculum, resource availability, and service outreach projects.

From De La Salle's Writings:

You are under the obligation to instruct the children of the poor. You should, consequently, cultivate a very special tenderness for them and procure their spiritual welfare as far as you will be able, considering them as members of Jesus Christ and his well-beloved. Faith, which should animate you, should make you honor Jesus Christ in their persons, and make you prefer them to the wealthiest children on earth because they are the living images of Jesus Christ our divine Master. By the care you have for them, show how truly dear they are to you.
(De La Salle – *Meditations* 80.3)

We are poor Brothers, forgotten and little appreciated by the people of the world. It is only the poor who come looking for us; they have nothing to offer us but their hearts, ready to accept our instructions. (De La Salle – Meditations 86.2)

You are required by your work to love the poor, since the task you have in this work is to devote yourself to their instruction. Look upon them as images of Jesus Christ, and as those who are best disposed to receive his Spirit in abundance. In this way the more affection you show for them, the more you will belong to Jesus Christ.
(De La Salle – *Meditations,* 173.1)

You have the happiness to labor for the instruction of the poor and to be engaged in a work which is esteemed and honored only by those who have a truly Christian spirit. Thank God for having placed you in so sanctifying a state, and one providing for the sanctification of others, which nevertheless has nothing attractive to others, and even gives those who labor in it frequent occasions to be humiliated.
(De La Salle – *Meditations,* 113.1)

You will give account to God... whether you have taught your disciples the things in the catechism that they should know according to their age and ability; whether you have not neglected some students because they were the slowest, perhaps also the poorest; and whether you did not show favoritism toward others because they were rich, or pleasant, or naturally possessing more lovable qualities than the others.
(De La Salle – *Meditations,* 206.1)

From Institute Documents:

Programs [in Lasallian Schools] must be frequently examined to see that they correspond to real needs. Courses must be organized and educational standards set in such a way as to foster the human development of the poor, for whom the Institute has a special concern. Persons must be the center of educational systems rather than the prestige of some academic curriculum. (*Declaration,* 31.2)

The purpose of this Institute is to give a human and Christian education to the young, especially the poor, according to the ministry which the Church has entrusted to it. (1987 *Rule,* Article 3)

Personal Follow-up Questions:

1) How does the voice of the poor join into the significant conversations in which I participate at my school?

2) What is the greatest challenge that I face in listening to the poor?

3) Where can I begin being more deliberate in serving the poor?

Working in Association:

The commitment to association is deeply ingrained in the fabric of the Lasallian heritage. From the very beginning, De La Salle came to realize that the schools would become successful and stable only to the extent that the teachers were united with a common vision, a shared dedication, and a supportive community. From the first retreat that he gave them in his house in 1681 to his last general assembly with them in 1717, he worked to knit his teachers into a religiously animated group of Christian educators who worked in, with, and through association.

The idea of association came to be applied in a variety of contexts. At first, the word described an effort to run each school with at least two teachers and not individually as the Schoolmasters did. Policies and procedures were shared as a result, and resources such as *The Conduct of Schools* emerged out of the common experience of teaching. When De La Salle and two Brothers took the "heroic vow" in 1691 to "associate" for the establishment of the Institute even if they had to beg for alms and to live on bread alone, "association" was not so much for the work of education as it was for seeing that the group survived and became established. Three years later, when twelve Brothers and De La Salle took perpetual vows, one of the vows was that of "association" to keep gratuitous schools. This last understanding of association is echoed in the Brothers vow formula of today.

The experience of association is also found on many levels. The early Brothers lived in a common house centrally situated among several schools, and established practices that would deepen their association (monthly letter to De La Salle, "Visitors" to groups of houses in one region, a yearly retreat). Classes in the schools were taught as an entire group, with appropriate structures to address individual abilities and with subject-specific advancement. Students found that they all had the same expectations placed on them, regardless of their social status. They worked together, prayed together, and grew into Christian maturity together. In the Christian School, education happened together.

The future of association among Lasallian institutions is vibrant and strong. The global, multi-national nature of this education–without–borders is enhanced every day by advancing globalization and technology. Brothers and Partners find their association strengthened in their common pursuit of educating the young, especially the poor. And Brothers communities increasingly realize their animating role within the schools, an animation arising out of their own unique life of consecrated association.

Association is not something that any of us may take for granted; it is something that each of us may take for real. All it takes is a decision to see that, for us, others do have a real voice, and those voices together make a real difference in what we do.

Consequences for taking such a commitment seriously: **students** would work in cooperation with others in the attainment of their education, cultivating an associative sense through collaboration; **teachers** would engage in cooperative activities targeting specific student's needs, mutual faculty formation projects, and common interests on a local, state, national, or international level; the **teacher-student relationship** would be committed to achieving common goals, with teachers and students accountable to one another for their appropriate responsibilities; the **activity of teaching** would actively engage students as participants in the teaching / learning dynamic and would pursue teaching as a cooperative art;

and **the school** would include faculty, students, parents, pastors, and alumni in its educational protocol and interact with other Lasallian schools, Catholic schools, and local, national, and international educational organizations.

From De La Salle's Writings:

Statements applying to the Brothers community, but also very applicable to any form of association:

Union in a community is a precious gem, which is why Our Lord so often recommended it to his disciples before he died. If we lose this, we lose everything. Preserve it with care, therefore, if you want your community to survive.
(De La Salle – *Meditations,* 91.2)

A community without charity and union is a hell: one grumbles, another slanders his Brother because of the ill-will he feels toward him, another gets angry because someone has irritated him, another complains to his superior about what one of his Brothers has done to him. In short, all one hears is accusations, murmuring, and backbiting, which of course cause much irritation and disquiet.

The only remedy for all these disorders is union and charity, because, as Saint Paul says, charity is patient. This holy apostle even desires that the patience which is the result of charity should go so far as to endure all things. Whoever says all does not except anything.

If, then, we have charity and union with our Brothers, and since we should endure all things from everyone, we can no longer say: I cannot put up with this from that person; I cannot stand such a defect in this other one; he will have to give in to my whims or my weakness in something. To speak like this is not to endure all things from everyone. Think carefully over this maxim and practice it exactly.
(De La Salle – *Meditations,* 65.1)

From Institute Documents:

Shared mission, as the very words themselves suggest, demands a process of growth in unity, in *communion* (literally in its root sense of *united with*), between persons who share the same mission. This process of communion requires the development of links of unity, of communication, unified objectives, common actions, and good personal relationships in the same Lasallian tradition which brought the Brothers to make a vow of association among themselves so as to maintain the schools *"together and by association."*

Association, such as it was lived by the Brothers, had a deep impact on the organization and functioning of their schools. It was a decisive factor in helping their cohesion, efficiency and creativity. Today, under new forms still to be invented, the same spirit of association should continue to inspire and give life to the Lasallian Schools where Lasallian partners are the great majority. The challenge now is for the Brothers and all other Lasallian educators to discover together in open dialogue how to found and promote in new foundations the associative dimensions of their commitment on behalf of the human and Christian education of the young, especially the poor. (*Shared Mission Document,* 3.31)

Personal Follow-up Questions:

1) How do you see "association" happening in the way your school does business?

2) What areas of your school reflect a true sense of association that's not just written down?

3) Where might you find the voiceless ones that those in your school need to hear?

Expressing a Lay Vocation:

Vatican II described the laity as those "who by Baptism are incorporated into Christ and integrated into the People of God, are made sharers in their particular way in the priestly, prophetic and kingly office of Christ, and have their own part to play in the mission of the whole Christian people in the Church and in the world." *(Lumen Gentium, 31)* The Lasallian commitment to education as a lay vocation highlights 1) a solidarity among those who participate in the church as non-ordained members, and 2) a recognition of the privileged calling embedded in the teaching vocation.

One of the most frequent questions that Brothers hear from parents or acquaintances who know them enough to ask the question, but not enough to know the answer, is "Why didn't you go all the way and become a priest?" Their short answer is usually, "Because I didn't have a vocation to the priesthood." Further discussion brings out the fact that the Brothers' vocation is a vocation to educational ministry, not to sacramental ministry. It is a lay vocation that has more in common with the people in the pew than with the pastor in the parish.

De La Salle established a teaching order of men who were to be neither "seculars" nor "clerics." They were to be dedicated to teaching as "Brothers," consecrated to procuring God's glory and the salvation of the young through the ministry of Christian and human education while keeping some distance from the hierarchical structure of the church. Brothers were not to be involved in any way in clerical affairs, from knowing Latin to leading the singing in parishes. Their place was with the students. The Brothers' communal prayer was not the recitation of the Divine Office but rather those prayers recommended by the church for all its members. The Brothers' posture *vis-à-vis* the church was substantially the same as that of their students and parents. In this way, they provided a convincing example of Christian virtue to all with whom they came in contact. De La Salle and the Brothers so situated themselves and their lives that all they did illustrated the vocation of Christian life for all the laity.

There have been, and are, religious orders that combine the roles of priest and schoolmaster (Jesuits, Salesians, Benedictines, Dominicans, Franciscans, and so on), but most of these don't devote themselves exclusively to education, nor are their members exclusively, or essentially and finally, school people. To some, that makes all the difference; not so much in terms of educational quality as in terms of educational momentum. There's a whole bunch of history, heritage, commitment and vocation riding on what happens in all the nooks and crannies of a Lasallian school. In a place where everything makes a difference, the value of the teaching encounter is what a Lasallian educator holds onto as his or her touchstone.

On a practical level, this lay character allows for, encourages, and empowers the sense of companionship that is so often cited by students and alumni. There is a down-to-earthness that characterizes the relationships found within a Lasallian school. At the same time, there is a care for one another that is similar to that of an extended family. As Gerald Haslam, an essayist, wrote when he unexpectedly encountered two others at a radio station who had gone to Lasallian schools, "That unexpected coincidence immediately changed our relationship because being a Brothers' Boy (a former popular term for an alumnus) is one of those special categories of experience that does not fade, that brings with it a range of shared experience and of pride. Like being a Marine or a mother, it sticks." The fact that this sense of solidarity comes from an experience that appreciates the lay vocation is part of what makes it stick.

Consequences for taking such a commitment seriously: **students** would become aware of their calling in the church and discover what it means to be identified with a particular parish, diocese, and denomination; **teachers** would develop an awareness of the dignity of the teaching vocation and model the identity of a lay person in the church; the **teacher-student relationship** would be modeled on discipleship, appropriate and respectful but personable and warmhearted, with a familial down-to-earth quality; the **activity of teaching** would retain an awareness of the ongoing responsibility of shaping the students' mature spiritual identity; and **the school** would share its concerns and activities as an active participant in the lay community, the parishes, its own parish, and the diocese.

From De La Salle's Writings:

You must, then, look upon this work entrusted to you by pastors, by fathers and mothers, as one of the most important and most necessary services in the church. For you lay the foundation for the building of the church. (De La Salle – *Meditations* 199.1)

Consider that you are working in your ministry for the building of the church through your teaching of the children whom God has entrusted to your care. These children are becoming a part of the structure whose foundation was laid by the holy apostles. For this reason you must fulfill your ministry as the apostles fulfilled theirs. . . . You are successors to the apostles in their task of catechizing and teaching the poor. (De La Salle – *Meditations* 200.1)

Reflect on what Saint Paul says, that God has established in the church apostles, prophets, and teachers, and you will be convinced that He has also established you in your ministry. The same saint gives you another expression of this when he says that there are different gifts, different ministries, and that to each person the manifestation of the Spirit is given for the common good, that is, the good of the church. (De La Salle – *Meditations* 201.1)

You must also show the church what love you have for her and give her proof of your zeal, since it is for the church (which is the body of Christ) that you work. You have become her ministers through the commission God gave you to preach His word to these children. (De La Salle – *Meditations* 201.2)

From Institute Documents:

The religious life of the brother represents one of the possible ways of being a layman in the Church. In fact, "the religious state of life is not an intermediate one between the clerical and lay states. Rather, the faithful of Christ are called by God from both these latter states of life so that they may enjoy this particular gift in the life of the Church and thus each in his own way can forward the saving mission of the Church" [*Lumen Gentium,* 43]. Thus the brother's religious life "does not belong to the hierarchical structure of the Church; nevertheless it belongs inseparably to her life and holiness." [*Lumen Gentium,* 44] (*Declaration,* 16)

"An understanding of this new reality demands a change of mentality quite as much among lay people as among the Brothers so that shared mission can be accepted as a gift of God which commits all engaged in it to develop it for the good of the common mission, the Christian education of the poor." (*Shared Mission Document,* 3.12)

Ever since the time of their foundation, the Brothers have contributed to the promotion of the Christian laity, especially among those educators who want their professional work to be a form of gospel ministry.

The Brothers gladly associate lay persons with them in their educational mission. They provide, for those who so desire, the means to learn about the Founder and to live according to his spirit.

The Brothers cooperate in forming Christian teachers. They help them to develop their professional competence and also to become increasingly involved in the work of the Church and in the field of education. (1987 *Rule,* Article 17)

Personal Follow-up Questions:

1) What do I see as my mission in the church?

2) Where do I exercise my identity as a lay person in the church most effectively?

3) How can I begin to appreciate more fully what it means to be a lay person in my religious community?

Here, then, are fifty particularized educational articulations of operative commitments arising out of the Lasallian heritage, divided among ten basic operative commitments and five operational aspects of the Lasallian school.

One must look at this collection of Lasallian commitments as a dynamic, integrative totality that would be virtually useless for delineating "Lasallian" characteristics without the active involvement of all of its aspects. They function in cooperation with one another, mutually shaping their particular emphases so as to form a single identity, a commonly shared Lasallian school character evident in the student, the teacher, the teacher-student relationship, the activity of teaching, and the school in general.

The school's explicit activities are filtered through each of the commitments and are individually colored thereby. Further subdivisions of each activity are similarly subject to these same commitments. For example, a schoolwide prayer service, from planning meeting to execution would each include components that reflect every one of the Lasallian operative commitments. Each commitment would not be engaged in exactly the same way, or with exactly the same emphasis, but all would be involved in some way if that activity is to be one that shares in the school's Lasallian spirituality. The challenge, as always, is to bring these Lasallian operative commitments to realization in the touching of hearts.

The simple and minimalist approach to the incorporation of Lasallian sensibilities would be to ask key questions of any Lasallian school situation or activity. These key questions, drawn from the commitments, focus on the considerations emphasized by the Lasallian tradition. As long as one has more than a passing acquaintance with De La Salle, his major convictions and his general history, these questions will quickly establish the degree to which the various aspects of an activity incorporate Lasallian school commitments. The questions are:

- Does the situation or activity look at everything with the eyes of faith, do everything in view of God, and attribute all to God?
- Does the situation or activity show a trust in Providence? Is it guided by an openness to God's will?
- Does the situation or activity proceed with creativity and fortitude?
- Is the situation or activity planned, accomplished, and animated through the agency of the Holy Spirit?
- Does the situation or activity incorporate Christian paradigms and dynamics?
- Does the situation or activity arise out of practice and return to practice?
- Is the situation or activity focused on accessible and comprehensive education?
- Does the situation or activity include, display, and transmit a clear preference for the poor, for the disadvantaged?
- Is the situation or activity one that exemplifies and fosters a united vision and common effort?
- Does the situation or activity have a dimension that will help individuals enhance their understanding, appreciation, and involvement in the church as part of the laity?

Applied to Teacher Formation

The true measure of an effectively sustained Lasallian school is the degree to which its teachers function within common Lasallian commitments. Explicit and implicit means of introducing, fostering, and enhancing those commitments serve the final and proximate ends of the Lasallian school. Even a brief description of how each of these aspects might be realized for each commitment will make it clear that fulfilling all the commitments of a Lasallian school is by no means either simple or without effort.

The following examples are geared more toward those who are part of the general administration of the school. Other examples could be pursued that focus on the teachers, students, or further specific components of school life. Going through the process of applying the commitments to one's own particular school situation will begin to bring them to life.

Applying the ten commitments to the issue of teacher formation, these would be some of the consequences:

• **Centered in and Nurtured by the Life of Faith**
<u>To Introduce</u> – *Explicit:* provide good resources (all kinds) on De La Salle and on Christian life. *Implicit:* treat all religious activities with seriousness and enough time.
<u>To Foster</u> – *Explicit:* have an annual faculty retreat, focusing on the life of faith for a teacher. *Implicit:* have school-wide assemblies to listen to captivating people of faith.
<u>To Enhance</u> – *Explicit:* request volunteers to lead the prayer at faculty gatherings. *Implicit:* listen to one another's stories of faith.

• **Trusting Providence in Discerning God's Will**
<u>To Introduce</u> – *Explicit:* include providential perspectives at faculty meetings and personal evaluation conferences. *Implicit:* accept the need for "personal days" or "family days".
<u>To Foster</u> – *Explicit:* articulate the providential aspects of school situations, events, and circumstances. *Implicit:* maintain a calm demeanor in the face of school crises.
<u>To Enhance</u> – *Explicit:* include an end-of-year faculty discussion on the past and the future of the school. *Implicit:* view challenges as opportunities for finding God's guidance.

• With Creativity and Fortitude

<u>To Introduce</u> – *Explicit:* include one yearly unprecedented, creative, and well-prepared program or approach. *Implicit:* budget funds for student or faculty-led creative or challenging projects.

<u>To Foster</u> – *Explicit:* establish clear, fair, innovative and timely school procedures for both students and teachers. *Implicit:* brainstorm solutions at faculty meetings to address persistent situations.

<u>To Enhance</u> – *Explicit:* encourage qualified teachers to try out new programs or teaching methods. *Implicit:* foster alternative student education ventures (field trips, enhancement weeks, and so on).

• Through the Agency of the Holy Spirit

<u>To Introduce</u> – *Explicit:* begin each quarter or semester with a faculty prayer service on teaching, the students, and the school. *Implicit:* solicit candid input from new teachers about school life.

<u>To Foster</u> – *Explicit:* address a particular student's needs at faculty meetings, agreeing on specific common goals. *Implicit:* give students a voice in evaluating and developing school policy.

<u>To Enhance</u> – *Explicit:* address serious challenges as a group after invoking the Spirit's help in prayer. *Implicit:* develop effective methodologies for discerning individual vocations.

• Incarnating Christian Paradigms and Dynamics

<u>To Introduce</u> – *Explicit:* begin the first interview of a new teacher with a prayer. *Implicit:* provide opportunities and resources for discussing and learning about Christianity.

<u>To Foster</u> – *Explicit:* utilize Lasallian prayer forms and foster increased awareness of theology, morality, and so on. *Implicit:* provide guidelines, examples, and structures for class prayer.

<u>To Enhance</u> – *Explicit:* make school-wide Eucharistic services fully participative on many levels. *Implicit:* provide a prayer and a Christian life resource area for the school community.

• With Practical Orientation

<u>To Introduce</u> – *Explicit:* provide new teachers with a "how-to" guide to the school, including tips on teaching. *Implicit:* welcome and facilitate feedback regarding school structures.

<u>To Foster</u> – *Explicit:* include classes geared for those ending their formal education after graduation. *Implicit:* support the use of guest speakers, practicums, and field trips.

To Enhance – *Explicit:* require a practical component in the planning of each course or learning unit. *Implicit:* organize regular school-wide assemblies on practical topics.

• **Devoted to Accessible and Comprehensive Education**

To Introduce – *Explicit:* include principles from the Lasallian tradition in education during orientation programs. *Implicit:* provide creative student scholarships and keep the education of students (and teachers) as a top priority.

To Foster – *Explicit:* encourage interdepartmental cooperation, and programs focusing on the marginalized. *Implicit:* provide appealing assemblies for educational awards and contests.

To Enhance – *Explicit:* eliminate tracked classes in favor of in-class strategies for advanced learning. *Implicit:* ensure that classrooms and class resources are in top condition.

• **Committed to the Poor**

To Introduce – *Explicit:* distribute statistics on the economic and cultural breakdown of the student body. *Implicit:* participate and support student and faculty involvement in local charity efforts.

To Foster – *Explicit:* solicit contributions for a specific student's participation in retreats, club trips, and similar ventures. *Implicit:* encourage faculty gatherings that maintain a simplicity of style.

To Enhance – *Explicit:* provide an annual faculty-selected, faculty-sponsored full scholarship for a needy student. *Implicit:* establish cooperative projects with poor elementary schools in the area.

• **Working in Association**

To Introduce – *Explicit:* provide regular social events for faculty and staff, including their families. *Implicit:* include faculty room bulletin board space for each school subject and area.

To Foster – *Explicit:* provide structures for interdepartmental discussions at faculty meetings. *Implicit:* allow each teacher to attend a local conference in his or her subject area.

To Enhance – *Explicit:* invite coaches to attend and critique the classes of teachers and vice versa. *Implicit:* make the faculty lounge a hospitable place to relax, read, and converse.

• **A Lay Vocation**

To Introduce – *Explicit:* invite teachers to describe and pursue their role in the church as lay members. *Implicit:* encourage involvement in parish and charitable church work.

<u>To Foster</u> – *Explicit:* provide access to church resources, Catholic publications, and exemplary lay persons. *Implicit:* have non-sacramental school liturgies led by faculty members or coaches.

<u>To Enhance</u> – *Explicit:* invite faculty members to initiate school-wide charitable projects tied to church efforts. *Implicit:* allow teachers to take time off for church projects or programs.

Cautions

Two cautions about these ten commitments are in order. First, the richness of this model is its flexibility. One should not look at it as a definitive statement. The arrangement of these basic operative commitments represents one perspective of Lasallian components of pedagogical spirituality, authentic and viable to be sure, but nevertheless the view from a particular position in the Lasallian universe. Further relationships and alternate distributions of its elements may come to light as reflection, discussion, and common application within the real experiences of the schools rearrange or complement its present scope. Such a developmental process would follow the precedent established in the production of the *Conduct,* as well as resonate with several Lasallian commitments, and so would be true to the tradition inherited from De La Salle.

Second, one cannot expect a model such as this to particularize the specific practices that will realize these commitments unconditionally. The difficulty in describing distinctive aspects of an essentially comprehensive and dynamic reality is that, on the one hand, such descriptions on the popular level are often anecdotal, couched in stories or poignant moments, while, on the other hand, on the scholarly level they are expected to be universally applicable, couched in statements that include a wide spectrum of situations.

The difficulty of keeping these two levels of expression in balance reflects the essentially mysterious and tacit nature of the reality such expressions are striving to describe. One author, Herbert McCabe, has pointed to a similar phenomenon in reference to appreciating one of Shakespeare's plays. He writes that depths of meaning are not found

. . . in a play when you watched it for the first time; you have to learn to understand it, and you cannot take short cuts to the depth. . . . [A]s we understand a mystery it enlarges our capacity for understanding. . . . [W]hen it comes to reaching down to the deeper meanings, there is no substitute for watching or taking part in the play itself. The mystery reveals itself in the actual enactment of the play. It is very hard to put the meaning of Macbeth into any other words and that is why literary critics are always harder to read than plays; it all seems so much more complicated. This is not because critics are trying to make things difficult nor is it that the deep meaning is itself something complicated. It is something simple; the difficulty lies in bringing it up from its depth. When you try to bring deep simplicities to the surface you have to be complicated about them. If you are not, then you will simply have substituted slogans . . . for the truth. (McCabe, 1986, p. 56)

The Lasallian school similarly deals with "deep simplicities," more acquired through experience than through description, that have to be brought to the surface with some complexity—necessitating a certain amount of work on the part of the reader—so as to insure that they won't simply be slogans instead of the truth.

Each of the Lasallian school commitments does posit specific intentionalities that have real ramifications if taken seriously, but it would be presumptive to say, for example, that the Lasallian operative commitment to a lay orientation requires each school to have a social studies unit on the role of the laity in the church or insist that its teachers have read the documents of Vatican Council II. These may be the consequences that apply to a particular school in a particular situation, but one cannot say so here. The real work of practical implementation happens at the local level, where practices are located.

One *can* insist that the Lasallian tradition establishes the form, design, and character of specific practices. Indeed, that is what these ten commitments specifically propose. But just as one cannot say that a person will become authentically Christian by solely attending the Eucharistic celebration every day, although such a practice is one from which Christian identity no doubt benefits, so also one cannot say that a Lasallian school is so by having the faculty and staff read the biography of De La Salle, although such a practice may be one from which its Lasallian identity benefits. Therefore, particular practices that have been part of the Lasallian tradition are likely to be helpful in forming a school's identity (prayers such as "Let us remember that we are in the holy presence of God," practices such as having teachers start class with a short "reflection" on some Christian, moral, or personal disposition), but they will not by themselves introduce or encompass that identity. Such practices, if authentically appropriated, emerge from the heart of the Lasallian tradition, but their establishment within a Lasallian school must be in harmony with a host of movements that make up the totality of authentic Lasallian identity.

CONCLUSION

Perhaps the best answer to the question "What does it mean to be a Lasallian school?" is "A school that takes the Lasallian heritage seriously in everything that it does." What that looks like can now be answered in the language of the operative commitments: "A Lasallian school is a school that is attuned to God's living presence, trusts God's providence, operates with creativity and fortitude, cooperates with the movements of the Holy Spirit, incarnates Christian dynamics, strives to be practical, is devoted to accessible, comprehensive education, is committed to the poor, operates in association, and advances the role of the laity in the Church." It is the kind of place where the miracle of touching the hearts of students occurs directly, deeply and daily, across the board and at all levels.

Without doubt, it is possible to have competent and caring schools that know nothing of the Lasallian heritage. There is also a sort of "default" level of operation that almost any school, especially a Catholic one, can reach in due course. The bells ring, the students show up, the faculty gets paid, the board of trustees meets, the teams win their games, and so on. Few people would ask for more or look more deeply into what makes the whole thing work, and most people are perfectly happy if things went along that smoothly, without fuss.

In fact, if the truth be told, most parents of secondary school students are simply looking for a fairly secure environment for their sons and daughters where they will be well prepared for the college of their choice and receive a bit of moral training in the process. There are some parents who have themselves gone to Lasallian schools or have had other children attend them, and they have come to appreciate the "something" that makes Lasallian schools more appealing than others. But these parents are in the minority.

Where a particular educational heritage makes a difference is in the particulars, particulars that coalesce into a certain "feel" or "palpable tradition" a school carries through the years. And the Lasallian commitments outlined in this book speak to those particulars. They point to the "something" that takes the good education already happening and infuses it with catalysts, intentionalities, and priorities that are like the addition of spices to a good stew, giving a flavor only fully appreciated in the tasting or in hindsight. While some of the operative commitments may be more pronounced or more obvious than others in a particular school, in the dynamic, somewhat messy enterprise of education such distinctiveness is both expected and advantageous. Each school has its own character and each day brings with it new challenges and rewards. It is the thousand-and-one daily decisions that are made by those within the school that set its direction and provide its life. Insofar as Lasallian commitments form, inform, and transform those decisions, the school is being true to its Lasallian heritage, and individuals are able to bring to realization the miraculous touching of hearts.

Educators who are part of such an educational community, who live out the operative commitments of the Lasallian heritage and are able to touch the hearts of students will then say, "You want to know what a Lasallian school is all about? Come and see!"

touching minds and hearts

changing lives

ANNOTATED BIBLIOGRAPHY

Books

Aroz, Leon, Yves Poutet, and Jean Pungier.
Beginnings: De La Salle and his Brothers. Translated by Luke Salm. Romeoville, IL: Christian Brothers Conference, 1980. This small book contains much excellent material about De La Salle and his seventeenth-century French context. There is a detailed chronological order of the events in De La Salle's life that makes up the second part of the book.

Aumann, Jordan.
Christian Spirituality in the Catholic Tradition. San Francisco, CA: Ignatius Press, 1985. This is an accessible overview of the kinds of spiritualities the Catholic Church has produced and the nature of Catholic spirituality itself.

Bannon, Edwin.
De La Salle: A Founder as Pilgrim. (London: De La Salle Provincialate, 1988.) This short little book presents De La Salle's life in terms of several key decisive moments that shape his character and mission. It is based on the doctoral dissertation of Miguel Campos, FSC.

Battersby, William.
De La Salle: A Pioneer in Modern Education. London, England: Longmans, Green and Co., 1949. This book is somewhat dated and, frankly, presents De La Salle from a perspective that misses the radical nature of the kind of religious life and pedagogy with which De La Salle became associated. If read with a critical eye, it does give some good background material.

Battersby, William.
St. John Baptist de La Salle. New York: The Macmillan Company, 1957. Although this is an older biography of De La Salle in terms of modern scholarship, it is a well-written, scholarly account of the life and times of John Baptist de La Salle containing a wealth of informa-tion. Some scholars strongly disagree with some of its presuppositions and conclusions, and several key historical points are now known to be wrong. It should be read and taken as a 1950's biography with all that that implies.

Bedel, Henri.
The Origins (1651-1726): An Introduction to the History of the Institute of the Brothers of the Christian Schools. Translated by Allen Geppert, FSC. Rome, Italy: Brothers of the Christian Schools, 1996. This is the first of four volumes that will present a modern reading of the history of the Institute. De La Salle is obviously the primary actor in the story

until 1719 when the focus shifts to the Brothers as the principal actors. Bedel does an excellent job in 222 pages of situating the birth of the Institute and of the Christian Schools within the social, cultural, religious, and political currents of the time.

Bedel, Henri.
XVIIIth Century (1726-1804): An Introduction to the History of the Institute of the Brothers of the Christian Schools. Translated by Allen Geppert, FSC. Rome, Italy: Brothers of the Christian Schools, 1998. This is the second of four volumes that will present a modern reading of the history of the Institute. Bedel presents in these pages the story of the great expansion of the Institute in the Eighteenth Century and its near collapse during the French Revolution.

Berger, Robert.
Spirituality in the Time of John Baptist de La Salle. Landover, MD: Christian Brothers Conference, 1999. This work contains eight essays by internationally renowned Lasallian scholars. The essays provide an in-depth survey of all aspects of the spirituality which shaped De La Salle himself and his Institute. The encapsulate fresh and illuminating discussions of leading ideas at the heart of French spirituality and will inform Lasallian reflections concerning contemporary social situations.

Brothers of the Christian Schools.
The Rule of the Brothers of the Christian Schools. Rome, Italy: Brothers of the Christian Schools, 1987. This document represents years of work on the part of the Brothers, having gone through several revisions and based on a thorough consideration of key concepts, images, and words in the Lasallian heritage. It faithfully reproduces the charism of the Institute in contemporary language. Although much of it concerns the Brothers and their life, those sections regarding the mission of the Institute are very valuable resources for anyone associated with a Lasallian educational enterprise.

Bryk, A. S.
Effective Catholic Schools: An Exploration. Washington, DC: National Catholic Educational Association, 1984. This is a good, comprehensive resource book examining the state of Catholic education in the United States.

Buckley, Michael.
"Seventeenth-Century French Spirituality." *Christian Spirituality III: Post Reformation and Modern.* Editors, L. Dupré and E. Salieris (with J. Meyendorff). New York, NY: SCM, 1989. pp. 28–68. Here is a comprehensive, short introduction to the French School of Spirituality and the context which led to De La Salle's own spiritual journey. The article provides a good foundation for understanding many of De La Salle's spiritual ideas and suggestions, and puts several somewhat obscure practices into a better light.

Buetow, H. A.
The Catholic School: Its Roots, Identity, and Future. New York, NY: Crossroad Publishing Company, 1988. This book and the next one would be particularly valuable for anyone wishing to pursue the nature of Catholic identity in Catholic schools, including Lasallian schools.

Buetow, H. A.
Of Singular Benefit: The Story of Catholic Education in the United States. New York, NY: Macmillan Company, 1970. This book and the previous one would be particularly valuable for anyone wishing to pursue the nature of Catholic identity in Catholic schools, including Lasallian schools.

Burkhard, Leo.
Beyond the Boundaries. Lafayette, LA: New Orleans-Santa Fe Province, 1994. A very readable historical novel based on the life and work of St. John Baptist de La Salle. The book can be especially informative for the young reader as an introduction to the life and times of De La Salle. Includes illustrations from the motion picture, "Who Are My Own," starring Mel Ferrer.

Calcutt, Alfred.
De La Salle: A City Saint and the Liberation of the Poor through Education. Oxford, England: De La Salle Publications, 1993. This dense book is now the most comprehensive English biography of John Baptist de La Salle that we have. It is not easy to read, but it is eminently worthwhile. Those who really want to delve into De La Salle's life will find all the results of contemporary historical research into his life within this book.

Campos, Miguel.
"Introduction." *Meditations for the Time of Retreat.* Translated by Augustine Loes. Romeoville, IL: Christian Brothers Publications, 1975. pp. 1–44. Although this book is now out of print, copies still exist in school libraries, Brothers communities, etc. This is one of the best introductions to the meditations that De La Salle wrote and the spirituality that those meditations represent.

Campos, Miguel, and Michel Sauvage.
Encountering God in the Depths of the Mind and Heart: A Commentary on John Baptist de La Salle's Explanation of the Method of Mental Prayer. Translated by Oswald Murdoch, FSC. Rome, Italy: Brothers of the Christian Schools, 1995. An invaluable analysis of De La Salle's method of prayer, this book of 494 pages is a translation of *Cahiers lasalliens 50.* A "study guide" (photocopied booklet) for use by individuals or groups in the study of this book was prepared by William Mann, FSC, and Gerard Rummery, FSC.

Colhocker, Lawrence. Editor.
So Favored by Grace: Education in the Time of John Baptist de La Salle.
Romeoville, IL: Lasallian Publications, 1991.
This is another excellent background book. It is short and very
readable. There are some fascinating sections about education that will
provide both insight and astonishment about the Lasallian heritage.

De La Salle, John Baptist.
Collection of Various Short Treatises. Translated by W. J. Battersby.
Edited by Daniel Burke. Romeoville, IL: Lasallian Publications, 1993.
The "novices notebook" compiled over the years and intended to be
used in training the early Brothers, it is an anthology of contemporary
masters in the French School of spirituality, excerpts from the scriptures, and comments by De La Salle himself. It expresses the rigorous
side of seventeenth-century spirituality, but also shows De La Salle's
trust in Providence, concern for the poor, and exultation of the
ministry of the Christian teacher.

De La Salle, John Baptist.
Conduct of Christian Schools. Translated by F. de La Fontainerie and
Richard Arnandez. Edited by William Mann. Landover, MD:
Lasallian Publications, 1996. More than anywhere else, it is in this
volume that the educational genius and pragmatism of De La Salle
shines forth. It has served for three centuries as the basis for administering Lasallian schools and is universally held to be one of the classics
in the history of education.

De La Salle, John Baptist.
Euvres Complètes. Rome, Italy: Brothers of the Christian Schools,
1993. This is the complete set of De La Salle's writings in French. It is
some 1600 pages long and must be ordered from the Motherhouse of
the Brothers in Rome, Italy.

De La Salle, John Baptist.
Explanation of the Method of Interior Prayer. Translated by Richard
Arnandez. Edited by Donald Mouton. Landover, MD: Lasallian
Publications, 1995. Combining the best of modern Lasallian scholarship and an easy-to-read format with the genius and insights of De La
Salle into what the Brothers called "the first and principal exercise of
the Brothers," this is a useful volume for everyone, religious or lay,
intending to develop a systematic prayer life while engaged in the
apostolate of Christian education.

De La Salle, John Baptist.
The Letters of John Baptist de La Salle. Translated by Colman Molloy,
FSC. Edited by Augustine Loes. Romeoville, IL: Lasallian Publica-
tions, 1988. An entirely new translation of all the known correspon-

dence of De La Salle. Some 150 letters, including forty never before available in English, addressed to Brothers, members of his family, religious of other communities, and lay persons illuminate the character of De La Salle. This scholarly work includes extensive commentaries incorporating recent research.

De La Salle, John Baptist.
Meditations by John Baptist de La Salle. Translated by Richard Arnandez, FSC, and Augustine Loes, FSC. Edited by Augustine Loes, FSC, and Francis Huether, FSC. Landover, MD: Lasallian Publications, 1994. This book combines all of De La Salle's meditations in one volume. Written at various times in his life, these little meditations were intended to serve as points for the Brothers to consider in their daily prayer. Though reflecting the sometimes rigorous ideals and practices of the French School of spirituality, they offer interesting insights into the value system of the Founder, and serve as wonderful guideposts to anyone in the ministry of education. Accompanying commentaries form an excellent backdrop to the historical period and to the meditations themselves.

De La Salle, John Baptist.
The Rules of Christian Decorum and Civility. Translated by Richard Arnandez. Edited by Gregory Wright. Romeoville, IL: Lasallian Publications, 1990. The first edition of this book was published anonymously in 1703 for use as a reading textbook. Considering the nature and background of the urchins with whom it was intended to be used, one can only admire the idealism and goals of the early Brothers. The book went through over eighty-five editions and was still in use in the mid-nineteenth century. Some of the rules will amuse and some will surprise, but De La Salle's premise for decorum and civility is simple: we are all children of God, worthy of the respect we give and receive.

Deville, Raymond.
The French School of Spirituality. Translated by Agnes Cunningham. Pittsburgh, PA: Duquesne University Press, 1994. This book represents the more current, comprehensive treatment of the spirituality that formed De La Salle's spiritual outlook. As a full treatment of the French School's many dimensions, it is the best work in English. It contains a chapter about De La Salle.

Everett, Dominic.
John Baptist de La Salle's "The Conduct of Schools": A Guide to Teacher Education. Ph.D. dissertation, Loyola University of Chicago, 1984. This work gives an excellent overview of De La Salle's educational milieu and the contribution that he has made to educational history by the innovations that he and the Brothers introduced. It especially focuses on his contributions to teacher training, in which he was a pioneer.

Gallego, Saturnino.
An Introduction to the Writings of John Baptist de La Salle. Translated by Arthur Bertling, FSC. Rome, Italy: Brothers of the Christian Schools, 1993. This short introduction of 69 pages by the preeminent Spanish Lasallian scholar is a translation of the introduction of the second part of Gallego's two volume study on the life and thought of De La Salle.

Grass, Paul, Editor.
John Baptist de La Salle: Two Early Biographies. Translated by William Quinn, FSC, and Donald Mouton, FSC. Landover, MD: Lasallian Publications, 1996. This is a new translation of the very first biographies written of De La Salle's life, one is by his nephew, Dom François-Elie Maillefer, OSB, and the other is by one of the early Brothers of the congregation, Brother Bernard. Both biographies are valuable resources for serious scholarship, although their approach tends to be skewed with an eye toward eventual canonization.

Groome, Thomas H.
"What Makes a School Catholic?" in *The Contemporary Catholic School: Context, Identity and Diversity.* Edited by Terence McLaughlin, Joseph O'Keefe, SJ, and Bernadette O'Keefe. London, England: Falmer Press, 1996. This chapter gives a very good overview of what makes a school Catholic. Thomas Groome is best known for his work in religious education—his books, *Christian Religious Education* (San Francisco: Harper & Row, 1980), *Sharing Faith* (San Francisco, CA: Harper & Row, 1995), and *Educating for Life* (San Francisco, CA: Harper & Row, 1997) are standards in the field. In this article, he brings to the question of Catholic identity the perspective of one who has worked with religious educators for many years.

Hermans, Alphonse, and Michel Sauvage.
"John Baptist de La Salle: Founder of the Brothers of the Christian Schools (1651–1719)" Translated by Philip Smith & William Mann. *Lasallian Spirituality Workbook.* pp. 27–41. Landover, MD: Christian Brothers Publications, 1994. This is a foundational text for anyone interested in Lasallian spirituality. It provides the fundamental parameters within which Lasallian studies were initially pursued and continue to be pursued today.

Johnston, John, and members of the General Council.
The Lasallian Mission of Human & Christian Education: A Shared Mission. Landover, MD: Christian Brothers Conference, 1997. This work is addressed to all those who are presently involved in the Lasallian mission of education. It provides an historical overview of the Lasallian heritage from its beginnings to the present, the aspects that would characterize educational communities that follow the Lasallian mission, and a comprehensive foundation for the growth of the

common mission of Lasallian education. It is one of the most important works in recent times and essential reading for all those involved in Lasallian education today, Brothers and Partners alike.

Koch, Carl.
Praying With John Baptist de La Salle. Winona, MN: St. Mary's Press, 1990. This is a collection of prayers that use De La Salle's writings as their basis. It includes some good introductory material about him and his spirituality. The prayers help bring De La Salle alive for educators today.

Laube, Robert.
Pentecostal Spirituality: The Lasallian Theology of Apostolic Life. New York, NY: Desclee Company, 1970. This book takes a look at Lasallian spirituality from the perspective of the Holy Spirit's actions in the dynamics of Lasallian educational ministry. The book contains some interesting summaries of De La Salle's writings in this regard.

Lauraire, Léon, Raphael Bassett, Antonio Botana, Giampiero Fornaresio, Alain Houry, Luke Salm, and Lorenzo Tebar, Editors.
Lasallian Themes. Rome, Italy: Brothers of the Christian Schools, 1997. This is a collection of 99 articles in 3 volumes by leading Lasallian researchers from around the world. Articles vary in length from seven to fifteen pages on a host of topics of a historical, educational, theological and religious nature. The articles are reflective of current thinking in Lasallian studies.

Lewis, Warren Hamilton.
The Splendid Century. New York, NY: Quille, 1978. This is an enjoyable book to read. It provides some fine insights into life in seventeenth-century France and does so with wit and wisdom.

Loes, Augustine.
The First De La Salle Brothers: 1681 – 1719. Landover, MD: Christian Brothers Conference, 1999. This book distills Brother Augustine's lifelong research on the early history of the Institute into a comprehensive presentation on the first Brothers of the Christian Schools. The work is a documentary and chronology of the 250 Brothers who lived and worked with John Baptist de La Salle during the forty years that he dedicated to establishing the Institute.

Mann, William. Editor.
John Baptist De La Salle Today. Manila, Philippines: De La Salle University Press, 1992. This book is a compendium of articles dealing with John Baptist de La Salle and his context, both in the past and today. It includes a translation of the article on De La Salle written by Michel Sauvage for the Dictionnaire de Spiritualité (ed. M. Viller et al. 802–822. VII. Paris: Beauchesne, 1974).

Mann, William.
The Lasallian School: Where Teachers Assist Parents in the Education and Formation of Children. Narragansett, RI: Christian Brothers Provincialate, 1991. This is William Mann's doctoral thesis project. It presents a rationale for the involvement of parents and teachers working together to uncover the rich potential that Lasallian schools can have in the lives of children. Provided are a statement on the re-visioning of the Lasallian school today, an articulation of the key values and characteristics of Lasallian schools, and an overview of the current process of refoundation of which the Lasallian school movement is the most recent manifestation. Three workshops are included in the appendix.

Mann, William.
Lasallian Spirituality Workbook. Landover, MD: Christian Brothers Publications, 1994. In this book are collected a vast variety of resources, lesson-plans, worksheets, articles, and notes on the topic of Lasallian spirituality and seventeenth-century France. It is an invaluable resource for anyone interested in helping others to learn more about this topic.

Mann, William, with Henry Dissanayke and Isaias Tzegay.
Ambassadors of Jesus Christ: Prayer Meditations for Christian Educators. Rome, Italy: Brothers of the Christian Schools, 1995. This series of 35 prayer meditations were prepared to assist Christian educators who were looking for some help in learning a Lasallian method of personal prayer. The five page introduction explains the method; and the prayers focus on such themes as "a good shepherd," "ambassadors and ministers," "guardians and guides," "builders of the church," etc. Seven brief articles or "testimonies" written by Lasallian educators can also be found in this 111-page book.

McCabe, Herbert.
"A Long Sermon for Holy Week." *New Blackfriars 67* (1986). This article is included here because I quote from it in the book and some readers might want to know the specific reference. It was one of those articles that is hard to put down or forget.

Meister, Michael. Editor.
The Declaration: Text and Contexts Landover, MD: Christian Brothers Publications, 1994. This book contains the entire text of *The Brother of the Christian Schools in the World Today: A Declaration,* a pivotal statement from the 1960's, plus twelve extensive articles on that text. The articles address the text itself, the new contexts for the text, and the future of the text. Of special note are the articles by Michel Sauvage and Luke Salm, both of whom were intimately involved in the writing of the original text.

Mueller, Frederick.
"The Perceived and Preferred Goals of Principals, De La Salle Christian Brothers, and Lay Teachers in Lasallian Schools." Ph.D. dissertation, Boston College, 1994. This recently completed dissertation (not
yet published but available from UMI) looks at how principals,
Brothers, and lay teachers in Lasallian schools of the United States
have perceived particular school goals and how they have seen
themselves acting toward them.

Neuwien, R. A.
Catholic Schools in Action: A Report. Notre Dame, IN: University of
Notre Dame Press, 1966. This is an older look at what Catholic
Schools were about in the sixties, but there are still some very insight-
ful elements in it.

Palmer, Parker.
To Know As We Are Known. San Francisco, CA: Harper Row, 1983.
This is a wonderful little book that presents an educational spirituality
that is both accessible and full of wisdom. It is the kind of book one
would get either as a gift from someone who also loves teaching or
from an administrator who cares deeply about what one does in the
classroom. It is not an easy read in the conventional sense, but each
page is rich and worthwhile.

Poutet, Yves.
The Origins and Characteristics of Lasallian Pedagogy. Translated by
Julian Watson, Finian Allman, Celsus Clark, and John Wasch. Manila,
Philippines: De La Salle University Press, 1997. This very important
text is the most thorough contemporary analysis of De La Salle and
the educational principles that are associated with the movement he
began. It examines both De La Salle's biographical background, the
educational / pedagogical movements current in the seventeenth
century, the teacher training methods employed by De La Salle, the
principal characteristics of Lasallian pedagogy, and the special features
of the Lasallian method of instruction. An epilogue by Alain Houry
looks at the present situation in the Lasallian world.

Poutet, Yves, and Jean Pungier.
An Educator and a Saint at Grips with the Society of His Time. London,
England: Brothers of the Christian Schools – London District, 1979.
This is another excellent background book about De La Salle and his
times. It provides some essential insights into seventeenth-century
French society.

Pungier, Jean.
If We Were to Re-write "How to Run Christian Schools" Today? Translat-
ed by Oswald Murdoch. Rome, Italy: Brothers of the Christian
Schools, 1980. Although a bit dated by now, this book attempts to

take *The Conduct of Christian Schools* and translate it into modern terms. Those who read it will be tempted to do the same.

Pungier, Jean.
John Baptist de La Salle: The Message of His Catechism. Translated by Oswald Murdoch, Landover, MD: Christian Brothers Conference, 1999. This book combines an analysis of the major influences on De La Salle's catechetical work, *The Duties of a Christian to God*, with a presentation of the question-and-answer section of his catechism. De La Salle's convictions regarding the Christian life and his sensitivity to the capacities of young students are both in evidence.

Pungier, Jean.
Ministers of Grace: The Work of Christian Education According to St. John Baptist de La Salle. Rome, Italy: Brothers of the Christian Schools, 1980. This brief pamphlet describes the educator as a minister of God's grace to the students entrusted to his or her care. It speaks of the seven interior dispositions outlined by De La Salle as needed for Christian educators and places these in the writings of De La Salle and in Scripture.

Rayez, S.J., André.
"Etudes lasalliennes." *Revue d'Ascétique et de Mystique* 28 Jan-March (1952). This is a wonderful article written when contemporary interest in Lasallian spirituality began in earnest. It provides some excellent contextual insights for the life of De La Salle and the study of his works. An English translation will soon be available from Lasallian Publications in a collection of articles edited by Robert Berger.

Regional Education Committee of the Christian Brothers.
"Characteristics of Lasallian Schools." Romeoville, IL: Regional Education Committee of the Christian Brothers, 1986. This short booklet is a final product of a United States / Toronto Region process designed to determine what characteristics of Lasallian schools might be ascertained. It provides one answer to the question of Lasallian identity and, as such, is worth studying.

Rigault, George.
History of the Institute of the Brothers of the Christian Schools Volume I: The Religious and Educational Achievement of Saint John Baptist de La Salle. Translated by Edmund Dolan. Moraga, CA: St. Mary's College Manuscript, 1988. Although not yet published in book form, this manuscript provides a detailed, well-researched introduction to De La Salle and his historical context. For those who appreciate history written by an excellent historian, this manuscript is worth searching out.

Salm, Luke.
John Baptist de La Salle: The Formative Years. Edited by Joseph Schmidt.
Romeoville, IL: Lasallian Publications, 1989. The first 30 years of De
La Salle's life are the focus of this study, with particular attention to the
seminary education that preceded his ordination and the university
years that led to his doctoral degree. Based on the published research of
Brother Leon Aroz, this book describes the people, ideas, and experiences that influenced De La Salle before he became involved with the
teachers and the schools. The book takes contemporary historical
research and presents it in a very readable style.

Salm, Luke.
A Religious Institute in Transition: The Story of Three General Chapters.
Romeoville, IL: Christian Brothers Publications, 1992. Luke Salm has
been able to attend four successive General Chapters over the last forty
years. This gives him a unique perspective and insight into Lasallian
life as it went through the transition engendered by Vatican Council
II. This book is a fascinating chronicle of that journey.

Salm, Luke.
The Work Is Yours: The Life of Saint John Baptist de La Salle.
Romeoville, IL: Christian Brothers Publications, 1989. This book,
now in its second edition, is the standard popular biography of De La
Salle. It is written in an extremely accessible style and would unques-
tionably be the first book I would recommend to those who wish to
learn about Saint John Baptist de La Salle. If you haven't read it yet, it
should be the next book you read.

Salm, Luke, and Leo Burkhard.
Encounters: De La Salle at Parmenie. Landover, MD: Christian Brothers
Publications, 1983. What *Beginnings* did for De La Salle's early life,
Encounters does for the crisis of his later years. It centers around
Parmenie, a place of retreat in the South of France that De La Salle
visited while temporarily estranged from the Brothers late in his life.

Sauvage, Michel.
*Catechesis and the Laity: The Participation of the Laity in the Mission of
the Word and the Mission of the Teaching Brother in the Church.*
Translated by Oswald Murdoch. Sydney, Australia: De La Salle
Provincialate, 1991. This is the translation in 358 pages of sections
four and five of an important work by Michel Sauvage published in
France in 1962. Its footnote references to the *Meditations* of De La
Salle are particularly valuable.

Sauvage, Michel.
"The Gospel Journey of John Baptist de La Salle." *John Baptist de La
Salle Today.* Edited by William Mann. Manila, Philippines: De La Salle

University Press, 1992. pp. 24–57. This is truly one of the most captivating short introductions to the spiritual journey of John Baptist de La Salle. Within a short period of five years, De La Salle is shown to be led by the Holy Spirit and providential events to respond more and more deeply to the Gospel's insistent call.

Sauvage, Michel, and Miguel Campos.
Announcing the Gospel to the Poor. The Spiritual Experience and Spiritual Teaching of Saint John Baptist de La Salle. Translated by Matthew J. O'Connell. Romeoville, IL: Christian Brothers National Office, 1981. This is a substantial work that takes a deep look at the teaching and experience of De La Salle, specifying the ways in which the needs of the poor were addressed by De La Salle and the early Brothers. Its depth of analysis into the spiritual teachings of De La Salle, especially those regarding service of the poor, is unparalleled.

Schneiders, Sandra.
"A Hermeneutical Approach to the Study of Christian Spirituality." *Christian Spirituality Bulletin: Journal of the Society for the Study of Christian Spirituality* Volume 2, Number. 1 (1994): pp. 9–14. This article gives a good overview of how the word spirituality has developed over the ages and proposes the parameters for its application to contemporary experience.

Short, Gery.
Collection of Lasallian Readings: Summary and Bibliography. Napa, CA: De La Salle Institute, 1993. This privately published collection of readings assembles in one place a vast variety of workshops and presentations on Lasallian themes. It is one of the best resources available for providing input on which reflections about Lasallian topics could be based. Many of these articles are also available on the internet at sites focusing on the Lasallian world.

Thompson, William, Editor.
Bérulle and the French School. New York, NY: Paulist Press, 1989. This book gives a very good foundation for understanding the school of spirituality that forms the basis for De La Salle's own. By understanding this distinctive French perspective on Christianity and the economy of salvation, significant dimensions of De La Salle's own spiritual works may be seen in a deeper, clearer, and more historically accurate context.

Valladolid, Jose Maria.
Lasallian Chronology. Rome, Italy: Vol. 31 (1994) 3/3 of Lasalliana. This is a bound volume of 228 pages that lists in chronological order every known fact relating to John Baptist de La Salle from 455 AD, when the name "Salla" first appears, to 1950. It also lists all of the sources for each of the facts.

Van Grieken, George.
To Touch Hearts: The Pedagogical Spirituality of John Baptist de La Salle.
Napa, CA: De La Salle Institute, 1997. This is the expanded version of
the topic covered in this book containing a significant amount of
material that was left out. This fully footnoted expanded version,
privately printed, would be helpful to anyone who wants to find out
more about De La Salle's context, convictions, commitments, and
practices, and to anyone who will be involved in faculty development
programs, since it includes detailed suggestions for such programs.
Copies are available through UMI or by writing to the author at De
La Salle Institute, P.O. Box 3720, Napa, CA 94558.

Wright, Gregory. "The Splendid Century: The Historical Setting for
the Life and Work of Saint John Baptist De La Salle." *De La Salle
University Dialogue* Volume 26, Numbers 1–2 (1992): p. 1–30. A
short but well-done article on the context within which De La Salle
grew up and worked. This would make a very good introductory
article for a discussion about De La Salle and his times.

Wurth, Othmar.
John Baptist de La Salle and Special Education: A Study of St. Yon.
Romeoville, IL: Lasallian Publications, 1988. This book takes a close
look at what De La Salle and the Brothers accomplished at Saint Yon
in Rouen, particularly the innovative approaches they introduced to
deal with delinquent youth of their day.

Videos

The Purpose of Lasallian Schools.
Produced by Gery Short. Napa, California: De La Salle Institute.
(23:30 min) This four part video was produced to help Lasallian
educators, board members and others focus more clearly on the
mission of Lasallian education. The video is structured around four
themes: (1) an overview, (2) intellectual development, (3) social
awareness and refinement, and (4) spiritual growth. Each of the 5-8
minute segments is intended to be used independently and incorporated into a discussion or workshop. Guidelines for discussion and
suggestions for workshops are also available.

The Twelve Virtues of the Good Teacher.
Produced by Gery Short. Napa, California: De La Salle Institute.
(24:00 min) This five part video was produced to assist Lasallian
educators identify the characteristics of the good teacher, and a profile
of the model Lasallian educator. The video is designed around the
narrated commentary of Brother Gerard Rummery on the text *The
Twelve Virtues of the Good Master* written by Brother Agathon, the fifth

Superior General of the Brothers of the Christian Schools. A model faculty workshop for use with this video is provided.

To Shine in Youthful Hearts.
Produced by Miguel Rapatan and Colin Griffin for the Pacific / Asia Regional Conference (PARC), 1993.(30:00 min) Also distributed by De La Salle Institute in Napa, California, this video profiles the journeys of three Lasallians deeply involved in the mission of the Institute. Particularly well presented is the nature of the Lasallian mission in Asia, expressed by the spirit of non-Christian Lasallian educators, the loyalty of alumni, and the clear focus on service to the poor. This video is recommended for use with students, Lasallian educators and board members as an introduction to the multicultural character of the Institute as well as an expression of the lived reality of "shared mission."

De La Salle: A Reflection by Gerard Rummery, FSC.
Produced by Gery Short. Napa, California: De La Salle Institute. (6:30 min) This video is an excellent, short reflective consideration of the life and impact of John Baptist de La Salle. It is an answer to the question: "How would you briefly describe De La Salle and his work to a group of people who didn't know anything about him?" The video can be used with adults or students for educational or prayerful situations.

Insights into the Lasallian Heritage by Gerard Rummery, FSC.
Produced by Gery Short. Napa, California: De La Salle Institute. (58:30 min) Brother Gerard responds to nine questions which describe some basic features of Lasallian history, pedagogy and spirituality. The responses to the questions range in length from 3 to 8 minutes.

Classroom Management in Lasallian Schools.
Produced by Gery Short. Napa, California: De La Salle Institute. (24:30 min) This video was produced to serve as a tool to initiate practical discussions among faculty and staff about classroom management. The program is divided into five segments which highlight principles of the Lasallian heritage and classroom management: "Knowing students, Organization, Vigilance, Confrontation, and Punishment/Correction." A guide booklet with suggested activities is included.

The Spirit of De La Salle.
Produced by Gery Short. Napa, California: De La Salle Institute. (11:45 min) A relatively short presentation of the life story of John Baptist de La Salle with a special effort to describe important personal influences and experiences in his life. The program also presents the characteristics of the Christian Schools as developed and formed by De La Salle and the founding Brothers.

Internet

www.lasalle.org

> This is the international website for the Brothers of the Christian Schools and all those engaged in the ministry of Lasallian education. It is a site that is growing as quickly as the internet itself is growing. This site in Rome is mirrored in Napa, California at www.lasalle2.org for those living on the American continent.

www.cbconf.org

> This is the website for the United States/Toronto Region of Brothers and Partners in Lasallian educational institutions.

www.montlasalle.org

> This is the website of the author of this book and contains a variety of resources in the area of Lasallian education and spirituality.

APPENDIX

Ten Commitments of Lasallian Schools

Lasallian pedagogical spirituality calls forth ten basic operative commitments that are based on foundational Lasallian convictions and manifested in consistent practices. Each commitment is presented in the form of an attribute or a quality of a Lasallian school.

1) **Lasallian Schools are Centered on the Life of Faith**
   De La Salle's overriding concern in all that he did was the life of faith, the reality of God's saving presence in the midst of daily experience. Lasallian teachers readily share their faith life with their students, both in their zeal for education and in their daily personal encounters. In a Lasallian school God's presence gradually becomes an evermore living and appreciated reality.

2) **Lasallian Schools Trust God's Providence**
   De La Salle confidently rested in a complete and radical trust in God's providential care for him, for the Institute, and for its work of education. Lasallian teachers share this radical trust by recognizing God's face in every school or classroom situation. In a Lasallian school, self-sufficiency is not the final voice. The work is God's work, first and last.

3) **Lasallian Schools Operate With Creativity and Fortitude**
   De La Salle's commitment to the Christian Schools led him to make bold, creative moves in response to God's Will. Lasallian teachers demonstrate the creativity of God's Love through their daily resourcefulness and resilience, imagination and determination, ingenuity and persistence. In a Lasallian school the continual pursuit of innovative educational programs is the rule, not the exception.

4) **Lasallian Schools Cooperate With the Action of the Holy Spirit**
   De La Salle often prayed to the Holy Spirit for guidance and urged his teachers to do the same. Christ's life is brought into the school by Lasallian teachers who are animated by the Spirit and willing to act accordingly. In a Lasallian school, the challenging, unpredictable, hidden life of the Spirit is given attention and heeded.

5) **Lasallian Schools Incarnate Christian Dynamics**
   De La Salle educated the young in order to make God's saving presence an active reality in their lives. Lasallian teachers seek and reveal God's presence in the minutiae of the exercise of their ministry. In a Lasallian school, Gospel maxims and Gospel norms provide the basis upon which its organizational and relational structure is built.

6) Lasallian Schools Strive to Be Practical

De La Salle recognized the real needs of youth and taught what they needed in order to function in society. Lasallian teachers prepare students for their vocation and profession, for their personal life commitments, and for service to society and the Church. Lasallian schools are realistic in their approach, methodology, and goals.

7) Lasallian Schools are Devoted to Accessible and Comprehensive Education

De La Salle provided an education that was available to all who desired it and that comprehensively prepared youth to participate in their society. Lasallian teachers affirm that education consists of more than facts, figures and skills; that true education forms a person towards Christian maturity and responsible character. Lasallian schools intentionally educate a diverse range of students and provide a wide-range, comprehensive curriculum.

8) Lasallian Schools are Committed to the Poor

De La Salle's concern was for the poor, the neglected and the overlooked. Lasallian teachers give greater attention to the neglected, to the marginalized, and to the less appealing students. Service projects and outreach programs bring the poor's voice into the lives of students. Lasallian schools are schools where programs that address the educational needs of the poor are an evident, clear priority.

9) Lasallian Schools Work in Association

De La Salle's efforts with teachers became more and more effective as he united them into a group with a common vision, a shared mission. Lasallian teachers come together as brothers and sisters associated with bonds of mutual respect, cooperation, generosity, patience, humor, and humility. Lasallian schools are not autonomous schools but operate in collaboration with others to accomplish their common ministry of education.

10) Lasallian Schools Express a Lay Vocation

De La Salle established a group of teachers who were to be dedicated to teaching as "Brothers" without directly being part of the clerical structures of the Church. Lasallian teachers reach out to their students in companionship, as older brothers and sisters, guiding their developing lives of faith and modeling the identity of a lay person in the Church. Lasallian schools advance the role of the laity in the Church by educating towards responsible, active participation in the life of the Church.

All of these commitments are mutually integrated, vital components of the experience of Lasallian education. They make up a unified set of dynamic characteristics that are integral to what it means to be Lasallian.

LASALLIAN MISSION AND VISION STATEMENT

Many institutions find it helpful to define themselves in terms of a Mission and Vision Statement. Were one to do so for a Lasallian school, the language for such a statement may best come from the ideas and principles expressed in the new *Rule* (1987) of the Institute, insofar as that *Rule* speaks about the mission and vision of the Lasallian charism. The tremendous amount of research and collaboration that was done in the formation of this *Rule* is reflected in the authenticity with which it speaks to the heart of what Lasallian identity is about, using ideas, images, and words that are integral to the Lasallian heritage.

Below is one articulation of what such a statement might look like.

Mission Statement

Lasallian schools are Catholic educational communities inspired by the vision of St. John Baptist de La Salle, providing a human and Christian education to the young, especially the poor, in solidarity with the living tradition of the Brothers of the Christian Schools.

Vision Statement

The spirit of those in Lasallian schools is a spirit of faith and zeal. They view all things with the eyes of faith, do everything in view of God, and attribute all to God. As cooperators with Jesus Christ, their faith, enlivened by the Holy Spirit, kindles an ardent zeal for the salvation of those confided to their care.

The principal function of those in Lasallian schools consists in the work of evangelization and catechesis through human and Christian education, determined to make the means of salvation available to young people, especially the poor, through a quality education and by an explicit proclamation of Jesus Christ. The school's activities focus on growth in faith and integrate the effort of human advancement with the announcement of God's word in a pedagogy characterized by personal companionship and the consistent promotion of justice, especially in regards to the poor. A spirit of prayer and an attentiveness to the presence of God animate the Lasallian school's identity. School personnel strive to touch the hearts of students, participating in a common mission. As ambassadors of Jesus Christ, they look upon their professional work as a ministry, opening others to the riches of God's grace and helping them to discover, appreciate and assimilate both human and gospel values.

Lasallian schools operate together and by association, collaborating with all members of the educational community to spread the gospel through education among all cultures and peoples. The vitality of the Lasallian school comes from the quality and fidelity of each of its members. All those involved in the mission of the Institute work in solidarity with each other, both as individuals and as groups, in order to accomplish the world-wide work of education in the light of Providence and a common Lasallian spirituality.

GLOSSARY OF LASALLIAN TERMS

SPECIALIZED TERMS IN LASALLIAN USAGE

The following glossary is a kind of dictionary of terms that might not be familiar to everyone associated with a Lasallian school. The words have to do mostly with Church and Institute matters and are in effect technical. The succinct descriptions offered here are meant to be brief but accurate and helpful for communication. The asterisk (*) is meant to indicate that the word so marked is treated elsewhere in the glossary.

A note about the name of John Baptist de La Salle: There are four ways in which his name is commonly spelled: (1) the name "De La Salle" is spelled with all the words capitalized; (2) in the longer "Saint John Baptist de La Salle" or "John Baptist de La Salle" the "de" is not capitalized [that word is pronounced more like "duh" than like "day"]; (3) when using "Saint La Salle," the "de" is left out entirely; and (4) in speaking about something associated with the heritage of De La Salle, we use the word *Lasallian* [not spelled LaSallian or La Sallian].

Affiliated Member: a man or woman formally inducted into a special group of those who have served Lasallian* ideals in some extra-ordinary way; the member may put initials AFSC after his or her name to indicate, Affiliated Brother* of the Christian Schools.

Apostolate: a specific kind of work to which the Church sends people and institutions as a mission*.

Aspirants: those who are seriously considering, usually in a non-residency program, whether or not they are called by God to become Christian Brothers*.

Assembly: A convention for Brothers* and colleagues from the whole Region* that occurs every few years as organized by those in the Region*.

Benefactor: a man or woman formally given this title for rendering extraordinary material help to the work of the Institute*.

Brothers: name given to official members of the Brothers of the Christian Schools and widely used in other male religious institutes* some of which may also, unlike the Christian Brothers, have priests* (mostly known as "Fathers") as official members.

Campus Ministry: a program of activities in a secondary school or college that oversees the liturgical life of the school and fosters Christian service and spirituality.

Canon Law: the *Code of Canon Law* (latest revision published in 1983) contains some 1680 canons or official regulations governing Roman Catholic cardinals, bishops, priests, Brothers*, Sisters, institutes*, laity, parishes, schools, sacraments, etc.

Canonical: an adjective used to describe any person or action that conforms to the requirements of Canon Law*, such as a Visitor* or a formal visitation.

C A P: An acronym for Community Annual Program, it is a set of principles, policies, and practices renewed and revised each year at special meetings by the communities* in order better to adapt the *Rule* * and District* regulations to local conditions.

Charism: a grace or spiritual gift given to those in apostolic* or missionary work primarily to help others (not oneself); for example, the gifts of preaching, prophecy and healing are charisms; the term is sometimes extended from individuals to apply to whole institutes*.

C I L: acronym from the Italian for International Lasallian Center, a program of some months conducted at the motherhouse* to train Brothers* and Lasallian* Sisters from around the world in Lasallian spirituality.

Community: a religious* community is a canonically* recognized group of people belonging to a religious* institute* and living in the same residence according to the *Rule* * of that institute*; the building of residence is often called the community house. Sometimes the word community is extended to mean the whole of an institute*.

Congregation: often used synonymously with order* and institute* for an officially recognized religious group. (See the note under "Institute")

Contacts: Those who have an interest in the Christian Brothers and have indicated that they wish to remain in contact with the institute.*

Convocation: a gathering of Lasallian* educators, administrators, board members, students, and others associated with the educational institutions of a District*; somewhat like an assembly*.

Councillor: a Brother* whose office is in Rome at the motherhouse* and who is chosen to assist the superior general* and his vicar* in the leadership of the Institute*.

Deacon: a member of the clergy ordained to be of service to a parish or diocese* as preacher and as minister of some of the sacraments but not as celebrant of the Eucharistic Liturgy, or Mass*.

Declaration: *The Declaration* is a document prepared in 1966, before a revision of *The Rule* * by the general chapter*, in order to describe the spirit, purpose, and work of the Brothers*.

Delegate: the religious* superior appointed by the Superior General* to represent him in governing a delegation*; the local administrating Brother* is called president.

Delegation: a geographical area containing too few Brothers* to form a District* but with prospects of eventually doing so.

Diocese: An organizational division within the Roman Catholic Church that defines a geographical area under the religious jurisdiction of a bishop.

Director: the local religious superior of a community* with terms limited by Canon Law* or by *Rule* *.

Dispensation: a canonical* document which dispenses a religious* from the requirements of the vows* and returns that person to the secular state of life.

District: a geographical area in a region* containing enough Brothers* to form an official, canonical* administrative unit in the Institute* under the direction of a Visitor*.

District Council: a canonically required board of Brothers* advisory to the Visitor*; it has a majority of elected members and meets several times a year.

District Chapter: a policy-shaping body of Brothers* elected to nominate Visitors* and formulate legislative acts adapting the *Rule* * to local conditions; it meets normally every three or four years depending on the District*.

District Twining: a pairing of Districts* or Sub-Districts* for mutual support and assistance.

F S C: Initials put at end of Brothers' names to indicate membership in the Institute* called (in Latin) *Fratres Scholarum Christianarum* (Brothers of the Christian Schools) and known informally as Christian Brothers or De La Salle Brothers.

General Chapter: like a District chapter* this chapter is one that meets at the motherhouse*, representing all the Brothers* in the world; it makes appropriate legislation, and chooses the Superior General* for a seven year period.

General Councilor: one of at least six Brothers* elected by the General Chapter* to act officially as permanent advisors and assistants to the Superior General* during his term.

Generalate: the headquarters in Rome for the Brothers*, often called the motherhouse* or the center of the Institute* or Casa Generalizia.

Huether Workshop: a national gathering of Lasallian* educators originally organized by Brother Francis Huether to address educational concerns on an annual basis.

Institute: in the Church a term (more correct than the traditional terms congregation* and order*) used to refer to all forms of consecrated life whose members live in community under vows or similar sacred bonds; it includes groups of priests*, or male or female religious*, and sometimes others. [However, an incorporated institution, as in De La Salle Institute, is simply a corporation in civil law.]

> Note: At first, De La Salle used the term "community" to refer to the whole group of Brothers, not the local community, which was called "the house." From the time of the heroic vow of 1691, the term "society" was used. After the legal battles of 1704, with the requirements of letters patent to be called a society, the term "institute," already used since 1694, became more common. It was only after the acquisition of the Bull of Approbation from Rome in 1725, six years after De La Salle's death, that the Brothers received canonical status as a lay institute of pontifical right in the Catholic Church. And technically it wasn't until after the Code of Canon Law created the category of a religious "congregation" with simple vows in 1917 that the Brothers' Institute could be called "religious." Today, after the revision of the Code of Canon Law in 1983, the word "institute" is used to refer to all forms of consecrated life whose members live in community under vows or similar sacred bonds.

Jubilee: an anniversary celebration for Brothers* who had received the robe* twenty-five, fifty, or sixty (or even more) years earlier.

La Salle: John Baptist de La Salle, founder of the Brothers* in France, 1680; canonized a saint in 1900; declared by the Church in 1950 to be Patron of All Teachers of Youth.

Lasallian: an adjective used to describe whatever is in the Brothers' heritage or traditions as initiated by De La Salle*; more recently also used as a noun to name those who share in the mission and heritage of the institute*.

Lasallian Volunteers: lay men·and women, mostly recent graduates from the schools of the Brothers*, who donate one or two years of their time and service to schools and projects in various parts of the world.

Lasallian Youth: young men and women, usually of high school age, who work to advance Faith, Service, and Community within the school and within the local community, usually through various service projects and school-wide charitable events.

LI-NE: An acronym for the Long Island-New England District*.

Mission: from a Latin root meaning "send," this word includes the various works or apostolates* to which the Church sends people and institutions. According to the *Rule*, the mission of the Institute* is "to give a human and Christian education to the young, especially the poor, according to the ministry which the Church has entrusted to it." (Article 3) "By virtue of their mission, the Brothers establish schools and cooperate in creating educational communities inspired by the vision of St. John Baptist de La Salle." (Article 13)

Motherhouse: the headquarters or generalate* in Rome where the Superior General*, his staff, various offices, and facilities such as CIL* are located.

NARB: An acronym for the National Association of Religious Brothers*.

NCEA: An acronym for the National Catholic Educational Association.

Novice: a person who enters the novitiate*, receives the robe*, and undergoes a year-long program of spiritual formation prior to taking first (temporary) vows* and prior to proceeding to further academic and pedagogical training. (The term is used similarly in other institutes of consecrated life for both women and men.)

Novitiate: the program (or even the building) in which a novice* receives his (or her) training.

Order: a general term loosely applied to institutes* of consecrated life and to religious congregations*; formerly the term was officially used for those institutes* that had priest members and took what were called solemn vows*.

PARC: acronym for the Pacific-Asia Regional* Conference consisting of Districts* in New Zealand-Australia-New Guinea and Southeast Asia including Japan and the Philippines.

Partner: a term used to describe those engaged in the common mission* of Lasallian education.

Postulant: someone who is formally accepted as a residency candidate for possible entry into the Christian Brothers* and the novitiate*.

Provincial: the term used in most institutes* to describe the person whom the Brothers* call Visitor*.

Provincialate: the community* in which the Visitor* resides.

RCCB: An acronym for the Regional Council of Christian Brothers, a supervisory board of Brother Visitors* within the US / Toronto Region*.

Religious: word to describe that form of consecrated life recognized by the Church where priests*, Sisters and Brothers* take public vows* and live in community*. [Note: diocesan* priests* directly under a bishop do not belong to this category.]

Region: a geographical area officially designated as a union of several Districts* and generally chosen on the basis of contiguity and common languages. There are seven Districts* in the United States / Toronto region.

Robe: the official religious habit worn by Brothers throughout the world especially on formal occasions but replaced by other officially approved garb in various localities; it includes a special white bib called a *rabat* and is similar to that worn by judges and barristers in England. Similar garb identified various professional fields in seventeenth-century France.

Rule: a canonically* approved set of about 143 statements (with substatements) about mission*, duties, and practices that the Brothers* throughout the world adapt locally as directives for their communities* and Districts*.

Sangre de Cristo: Shortened form of the name given to the national retreat house sponsored by the United States/Toronto Region* for extended workshops and retreats, and located just outside Santa Fe, New Mexico. It is open to members of various religious institutes*.

SECOLI: an acronym for Service de Cooperation Lasallienne Internationale, an agency at the motherhouse* which coordinates contributions to various apostolates* around the world.

SIEL: An acronym from the Italian for International Session of Lasallian Studies, an occasional program of studies in Lasallian spirituality and pedagogy at the motherhouse*.

Shared Mission: the term used to describe the common apostolate of Lasallian education among Lasallian partners*. The growing preference among Lasallian partners is to use only the term *mission** when speaking about their educational work.

Sub-District: a group of communities*, generally in missionary areas, not numerous enough to form a delegation* or a full District* often presided over by an Auxiliary Visitor*.

Superior General: the highest officer of the Institute* with canonical* rights and duties; he works out of the generalate in Rome and is assisted by a vicar* and councillors*.

Vicar General: second highest officer of the Institute*, something like the senior vice president.

Visitor: the one primarily responsible for the District and the principal animator of a District* who is often called provincial* and has canonical* rights and duties. "He exercises his authority as a major superior in accordance with the norms of canon* law, the legislation of the Institute* and the directives given by the District Chapter*." (Rule, Article 132)

Vows: commitments of religious consecration taken by religious* and members of other forms of consecrated life and expressed in the Institute of the Brothers of the Christian Schools through vows of chastity, poverty, obedience, association for the service of the poor through education, and stability in the Institute according to the *Rule**. First vows, annual vows (or temporary), and final (or perpetual) vows are terms that respectively describe vows taken for one year at the end of the novitiate*, vows taken for one year and renewable on an annual basis until the time for permanent vows (generally at the age of twenty-five or after at least five years of annual vows.)

(This glossary is an edited version of a glossary by Br. Brendan Kneale, FSC)

INDEX

M